JIRA Agile Essentials

Bring the power of Agile to Atlassian JIRA and run
your projects efficiently with Scrum and Kanban

Patrick Li

BIRMINGHAM - MUMBAI

JIRA Agile Essentials

First published: June 2015

Production reference: 1220615

Published by Packt Publishing Ltd.
Livery Place
35 Livery Street
Birmingham B3 2PB, UK.

ISBN 978-1-78439-491-2

www.packtpub.com

Credits

Author
Patrick Li

Reviewers
Tejas Bhanuchandra Bhandari

Miroslav Králik

Mykhailo Moroz

Acquisition Editor
Sonali Vernekar

Content Development Editor
Arwa Manasawala

Technical Editor
Shiny Poojary

Copy Editor
Angad Singh

Project Coordinator
Shweta H. Birwatkar

Proofreader
Safis Editing

Indexer
Rekha Nair

Production Coordinator
Manu Joseph

Cover Work
Manu Joseph

About the Author

Patrick Li is a cofounder and senior engineer at AppFusions. AppFusions is an expert company that develops and packages integrated solutions for many enterprise applications and platforms, including IBM Connections, Jive, Atlassian, Google Apps, Box, Dropbox, and more.

He has worked in the Atlassian ecosystem for over 8 years, developing products and solutions for the Atlassian platform and providing expert consulting services. He is one of the top contributors to the Atlassian community, providing answers and advice on forums such as Atlassian Answers and Quora.

He has extensive experience in the design and deployment of Atlassian solutions from the ground up, and customizing existing deployments for clients across vertical markets, such as healthcare, software engineering, financial services, and government agencies.

I would like to thank all the reviewers for their valuable feedback, and also the publishers and coordinators for their help and support in making this happen. Last but not the least, I would like to thank my family, especially my wife, Katherine, for encouraging me along the way.

About the Reviewers

Tejas Bhanuchandra Bhandari is a computer science graduate from Mumbai University. He hails from Mumbai and has also done his Masters in Computer Application from Mumbai University. He is an avid traveler and loves exploring new places and meeting new people. He has great passion for computers, which eventually became his profession. He is currently employed with Diebold, Incorporated, where he is working as a senior Java professional. He has vast experience of more than 5 years in software development. He has been actively involved in the end-to-end development of many Java-based applications. He has acquired expertise in project life cycle and is able to execute a project successfully from scratch. He is keen on learning and experimenting with new technologies.

Miroslav Králik is a young professional focusing on ITIL-based ITSM with a passion for helping clients succeed, and making products, services, and processes better. He is currently onboard a multinational integrated digital agency, where he leads a technical team and is responsible for EMEA web application maintenance and support services.

He has been using, administrating, and developing custom plugins and scripts for JIRA for 3 years at different companies.

Miroslav can be found on LinkedIn (`https://www.linkedin.com/in/mikralik`), or at `www.mkralik.com`.

Mykhailo Moroz is a certified Scrum master and software development engineer with 8 years of professional experience.

During his career, he has worked on varied projects from very small to very large companies, following different development methodologies starting from waterfall and right up to Scrum and Kanban.

His background includes deep knowledge in computer networks, programming, and test automation. Proper usage of tools such as JIRA has been helpful in the organization of work process and visibility, especially when a team is distributed across the world.

More information about Mykhailo can be found on his website: `http://mykhailo.com`.

www.PacktPub.com

Support files, eBooks, discount offers, and more

For support files and downloads related to your book, please visit www.PacktPub.com.

Did you know that Packt offers eBook versions of every book published, with PDF and ePub files available? You can upgrade to the eBook version at www.PacktPub.com and as a print book customer, you are entitled to a discount on the eBook copy. Get in touch with us at service@packtpub.com for more details.

At www.PacktPub.com, you can also read a collection of free technical articles, sign up for a range of free newsletters and receive exclusive discounts and offers on Packt books and eBooks.

https://www2.packtpub.com/books/subscription/packtlib

Do you need instant solutions to your IT questions? PacktLib is Packt's online digital book library. Here, you can search, access, and read Packt's entire library of books.

Why subscribe?

- Fully searchable across every book published by Packt
- Copy and paste, print, and bookmark content
- On demand and accessible via a web browser

Free access for Packt account holders

If you have an account with Packt at www.PacktPub.com, you can use this to access PacktLib today and view 9 entirely free books. Simply use your login credentials for immediate access.

Instant updates on new Packt books

Get notified! Find out when new books are published by following @PacktEnterprise on Twitter or the *Packt Enterprise* Facebook page.

Table of Contents

Preface

JIRA Agile or agile software development is a new and revolutionary way of developing software. Many organizations have adopted agile over the traditional waterfall model, as it lets development teams produce software with better quality, higher customer satisfaction, and improved efficiency. JIRA Agile brings the power of agile to Atlassian JIRA; the most popular enterprise issue tracking and project management system. It builds on top of JIRA, allowing you to leverage many of its customization abilities including workflows and custom fields.

With JIRA Agile, you will be able to enjoy all the features that you love in JIRA and also use Agile to manage and run your projects with an all new interface, as well as switch between the two when required.

What this book covers

This book is organized into five chapters, starting with an overview of JIRA Agile, how it fits in with JIRA, and how to install JIRA Agile. We then move on to introducing the two main agile methodologies, Scrum and Kanban, and how to use JIRA Agile with them. In the last chapter, we will go beyond the basics and look at ways to further customize JIRA Agile to bring out more value from it.

With each chapter, you will learn important concepts including the agile methodologies themselves and how JIRA Agile lets you take advantage of what they offer.

Chapter 1, JIRA Agile Basics, serves as a starting point for the book and aims to guide you through installing and getting JIRA Agile up and running. This chapter will also be a gentle introduction, covering basic concepts and terminologies used in JIRA Agile, laying the foundation for subsequent chapters.

Chapter 2, JIRA Agile for Scrum, covers using JIRA Agile for the Scrum methodology. Starting with a high level overview of Scrum, it describes how JIRA Agile can be used to run projects with Scrum.

Chapter 3, Customizing the Scrum Board, extends on the previous chapter by introducing some of the additional customizations available for running Scrum projects with JIRA Agile. This chapter covers some of the key customization options including board column layout and swimlanes.

Chapter 4, JIRA Agile for Kanban, covers using JIRA Agile for the Kanban methodology. This chapter starts with an introduction of Kanban and how to use JIRA Agile to run Kanban-based projects.

Chapter 5, JIRA Agile – Advanced, covers some advanced uses of JIRA Agile, including additional customization options, and how to integrate JIRA Agile with Atlassian JIRA and Confluence. By integrating JIRA Agile with these two applications, teams can be more effective at creating contents and reporting on project progress. This chapter also covers using third party add-ons for JIRA Agile, to extend its capabilities.

What you need for this book

Since JIRA Agile is an add-on extension to Atlassian JIRA, you will need a running installation of JIRA. You can download and install the latest version of JIRA from `http://www.atlassian.com/software/jira/download`.

For JIRA Agile, as well as the additional add-on Agile Cards for JIRA (used in *Chapter 5, JIRA Agile – Advanced*), you will be able to download and install them from inside the JIRA application. However, if your JIRA installation does not have access to the Internet, you can download JIRA Agile from `https://marketplace.atlassian.com/plugins/com.pyxis.greenhopper.jira` and Agile Cards for JIRA from `https://marketplace.atlassian.com/plugins/com.spartez.scrumprint.scrumplugin`.

Who this book is for

If you want to get started with JIRA Agile, and learn how to run your JIRA projects the agile way, then this is the perfect book for you. Perhaps you have used agile to run your projects before, or are just looking to try agile out, then JIRA Agile is the perfect way to get started.

You will need to be familiar with the basics of JIRA, both from an end user's and administrator's perspective. Experience with workflows, custom fields, and other administrative functions of JIRA will also be useful. Prior experience with JIRA Agile is not required, but is advantageous.

Conventions

In this book, you will find a number of text styles that distinguish between different kinds of information. Here are some examples of these styles and an explanation of their meaning.

Code words in text, database table names, folder names, filenames, file extensions, pathnames, dummy URLs, user input, and Twitter handles are shown as follows: "Make sure you do not remove the ORDER BY Rank ASC part of the query."

New terms and **important words** are shown in bold. Words that you see on the screen, for example, in menus or dialog boxes, appear in the text like this: "Click on the **Free trial** button for JIRA Agile in the search result list."

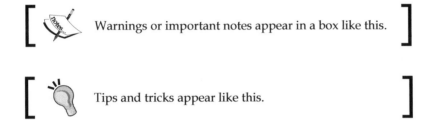

Warnings or important notes appear in a box like this.

Tips and tricks appear like this.

Reader feedback

Feedback from our readers is always welcome. Let us know what you think about this book—what you liked or disliked. Reader feedback is important for us as it helps us develop titles that you will really get the most out of.

To send us general feedback, simply e-mail feedback@packtpub.com, and mention the book's title in the subject of your message.

If there is a topic that you have expertise in and you are interested in either writing or contributing to a book, see our author guide at www.packtpub.com/authors.

Customer support

Now that you are the proud owner of a Packt book, we have a number of things to help you to get the most from your purchase.

Downloading the color images of this book

We also provide you with a PDF file that has color images of the screenshots/ diagrams used in this book. The color images will help you better understand the changes in the output. You can download this file from `https://www.packtpub.com/sites/default/files/downloads/4912EN_ColoredImages.pdf`.

Errata

Although we have taken every care to ensure the accuracy of our content, mistakes do happen. If you find a mistake in one of our books—maybe a mistake in the text or the code—we would be grateful if you could report this to us. By doing so, you can save other readers from frustration and help us improve subsequent versions of this book. If you find any errata, please report them by visiting `http://www.packtpub.com/submit-errata`, selecting your book, clicking on the **Errata Submission Form** link, and entering the details of your errata. Once your errata are verified, your submission will be accepted and the errata will be uploaded to our website or added to any list of existing errata under the Errata section of that title.

To view the previously submitted errata, go to `https://www.packtpub.com/books/content/support` and enter the name of the book in the search field. The required information will appear under the **Errata** section.

Piracy

Piracy of copyrighted material on the Internet is an ongoing problem across all media. At Packt, we take the protection of our copyright and licenses very seriously. If you come across any illegal copies of our works in any form on the Internet, please provide us with the location address or website name immediately so that we can pursue a remedy.

Please contact us at `copyright@packtpub.com` with a link to the suspected pirated material.

We appreciate your help in protecting our authors and our ability to bring you valuable content.

Questions

If you have a problem with any aspect of this book, you can contact us at `questions@packtpub.com`, and we will do our best to address the problem.

1
JIRA Agile Basics

Agile software development has been gaining momentum over the years as more and more people start to see problems with the traditional model, and the benefits agile methodologies bring. In agile, development happens in iterative cycles and improvements are made in each iteration. Feedback is gathered as early as possible, improving customer engagement and team collaboration. All of these actions help development teams to better anticipate and manage changes.

Atlassian, the maker of popular issue tracking software JIRA, recognizes the values agile can bring. It has become a leader in agile software development by coming out with JIRA Agile, a product that adds agile support to JIRA. In this chapter, we will introduce the basics of JIRA Agile.

By the end of the chapter, you will have learned:

- What JIRA Agile is
- The different options to install JIRA Agile
- The key concepts and terminologies
- Creating new agile projects with project templates

Introducing JIRA Agile

JIRA Agile, formerly known as GreenHopper, is a JIRA add-on that enables agile capabilities in JIRA. This does not mean you need to choose between JIRA and JIRA Agile. As we will see later in this chapter, JIRA Agile simply takes the data stored in JIRA, transforms and presents it in a way that makes it easier for you to visualize, plan, and manage your issues with agile methodologies such as Scrum. JIRA Agile supports two agile methodologies:

- **Scrum**: This is an agile methodology where the development team works iteratively to complete the project. Each iteration or sprint has a defined timeframe and scope. Scrum is most suitable for software development projects. You can find out more about Scrum at `http://en.wikipedia.org/wiki/Scrum_(software_development)`.

- **Kanban**: This is an agile methodology that emphasizes on just-in-time delivery by visualizing the workflow and tasks in progress. Kanban is most suitable for operation teams. You can find out more about Kanban at `http://en.wikipedia.org/wiki/Kanban`.

In short, the following list summarizes what JIRA Agile is and is not:

- JIRA Agile *is* an add-on for JIRA
- JIRA Agile *is* powered by new features and data stored in JIRA
- JIRA Agile *is not* a separate, standalone application
- JIRA Agile *does not* require you to be a seasoned JIRA user to use it
- As an end user, you can use JIRA Agile, almost independently, from JIRA if you choose to

Installing JIRA Agile

Before we can install JIRA Agile, we first need to make sure we have everything we need. Firstly, you will need to have an account on the my Atlassian website (`http://my.atlassian.com`). You should have an account when installing JIRA and the account should have your JIRA license. If you wish to try the product, you can sign up and create an account for an evaluation purpose.

The easiest way to get JIRA Agile is to install it directly from JIRA, via the **Universal Plugin Manager** (**UPM**). To do this, you will need to have an account with JIRA System Administrator global permission, and perform the following steps:

1. Click on the cog icon ⚙ from the top right-hand corner of the screen and select the **Add-ons** option.

2. Type in `JIRA Agile` in the search box and hit the *Enter* key on your keyboard. This will search Atlassian Marketplace and automatically find the latest version of JIRA Agile that is compatible with your version of JIRA, this is shown in the following screenshot:

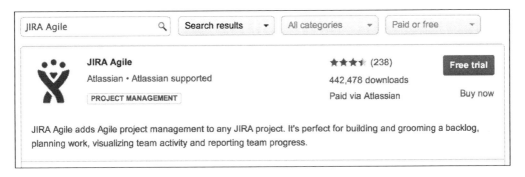

3. Click on the **Free trial** button for JIRA Agile in the search result list.

4. Review and accept the end user agreement from Atlassian Marketplace. Once you have accepted the agreement, JIRA will automatically download and install JIRA Agile for you.

5. Enter your Atlassian ID (your Mac account) when prompted and click on the **Log in** button, as shown in the following screenshot. This will automatically generate for you a 30 day trial license for JIRA Agile:

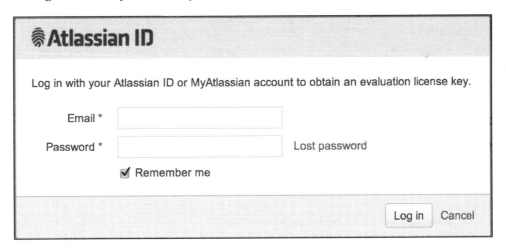

6. After the 30 day trial license has been generated and automatically applied, you will get a confirmation message similar to the following screenshot, indicating the version of JIRA Agile installed:

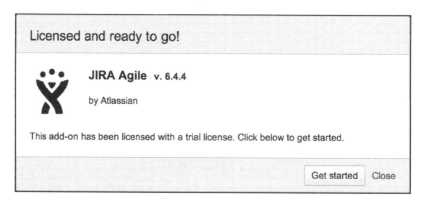

7. Click on the **Get started** button to take you to the **Getting Started with JIRA Agile** page as shown in the following screenshot:

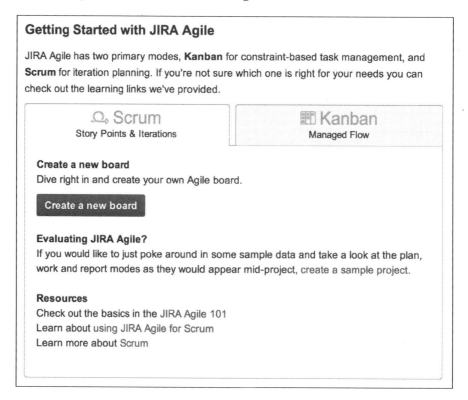

Manually installing JIRA Agile

As you can see, installing JIRA Agile is simple and straightforward. However, there might be times when you cannot use the **Universal Plugin Manager (UPM)**. In these cases, you will need to manually download JIRA Agile from `https://marketplace.` `atlassian.com/plugins/com.pyxis.greenhopper.jira` onto your local computer first, then upload and install it via the UPM.

You might want to do a manual installation if you need to install a specific version of JIRA Agile due to version compatibility issues or other bugs with the latest release. Another reason would be if your JIRA does not have access to Atlassian Marketplace due to network or firewall settings. To manually install JIRA Agile:

1. Go to the preceding link and click on the **Download** link to get the add-on file.

2. Go back to JIRA and click on the cog icon in the top right-hand corner and select the **Add-ons** option.

3. Select the **Manage add-ons** option from the left-hand panel.

4. Click on the **Upload add-on** link:

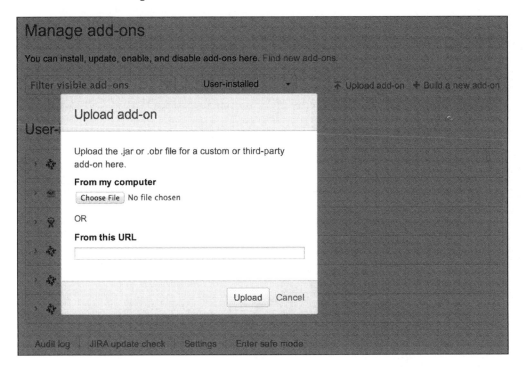

5. Select the downloaded add-on file, and click on the **Upload** button.

6. After you have uploaded the add-on, you will need to generate an evaluation license. You can do this by either going to `https://my.atlassian.com` or the Marketplace page and clicking on the **Try it free** button.

Understanding JIRA and JIRA Agile

If you have used JIRA before, it is useful to understand how JIRA and JIRA Agile work together as a whole. Firstly, as we have mentioned earlier, JIRA Agile is an add-on for JIRA, so it leverages many of JIRA's features. It also introduces some new features and concepts

The agile board

The agile board, or simply board, is a new user interface introduced in JIRA Agile. It is the main interface you, as the end user, will be using most of the time. If we use a real life comparison, the agile board will be your white board where you will place your user stories as post-it notes, which will be represented as cards. Essentially, you get the advantages of being able to visualize your backlog, as well as the added benefits of keeping track of changes and the progress of your tasks, along with reporting capabilities. For many teams, to keep using a white board is still very valuable, and we will look at ways we can combine both the white board and the JIRA Agile board in *Chapter 5, JIRA Agile – Advanced*.

In JIRA Agile, there are two different types of boards, one for Scrum and the other for Kanban, each with their own features. There is also a classic board, which is no longer under active development, so we will not be covering it. The following screenshot shows a sample Scrum board in the work mode:

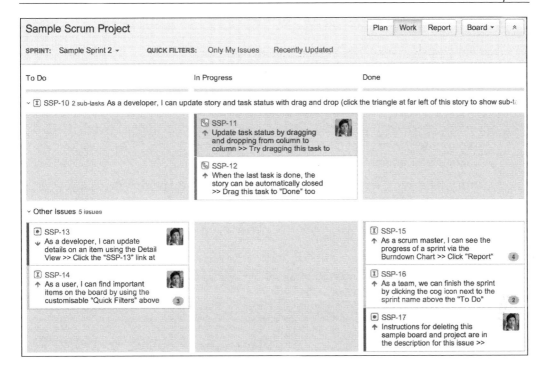

Card

A card is like a post-it note you would have on your white board. It captures the user story and represents the requirement or feature that is to be implemented. In JIRA Agile, each card is an issue in JIRA. The following screenshot shows what a card looks like in JIRA Agile:

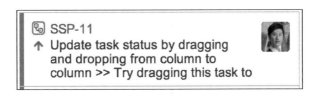

Issues and issue types

Every unit of work in JIRA Agile, such as a story or an epic, is an issue in JIRA. They are simply new issue types created by JIRA Agile when it is installed. The following new issue types will be added:

- **Epic**: This represents a big user story that has not been broken down into finer-grained requirements. In JIRA Agile, epics are usually used to define the "theme" for several stories that will be part of it, as well as modules or major components in a big development project.

- **Story**: This represents a single feature to be implemented. It is usually used to capture requirements from the end user's perspective. For this reason, stories are often written in non-technical language while focusing on the desired results of the feature.

- **Technical task**: This is a subtask issue type that represents the actual technical work that needs to be done in order to implement the story.

Filters and JQL

JIRA Agile is able to work on either one specific project, or multiple projects at once. When you want to have multiple projects, you will need to use filters to define what issues will be included. For this reason, understanding and being able to use **JIRA Query Language (JQL)** effectively can be very handy. You can find more information on JQL at `https://confluence.atlassian.com/display/JIRA/Advanced+Searching`.

Workflows

Workflow is the heart of JIRA and is what powers JIRA Agile in the background. As we will see in later chapters, JIRA Agile is able to integrate with your existing workflows, or adapt to and model after your development process. When you are just getting started, you don't have to know much about workflow as JIRA Agile will take care of it for you.

Using JIRA Agile project templates

To help you get started quickly, JIRA Agile comes with two new project templates, one for Scrum and one for Kanban. If you are familiar with JIRA, project templates let you create new projects based on pre-defined templates. So, when the project is created, it will have all the necessary configurations set for you, including:

- **Issue type scheme**: An issue type scheme that contains only agile-related issue types, such as story and epic.

- **Workflow**: A specially designed workflow to work with JIRA Agile that lets you easily move tasks on your board.

- **Screens**: A set of screens that contain necessary fields for working with agile, such as epic link to link stories to epics, and sprint for when tasks are added to Scrum sprints.

- **Agile board**: An agile board that is dedicated to the new project.

The agile board is a handy tool if you want to create a new agile project and get running straight away. To use these new templates, perform the following steps:

1. Select the **Create Project** option from the **Projects** drop-down menu.

2. From the **Select Project Type** dialog, select either the **Agile Scrum** or **Agile Kanban** template and click on the **Next** button:

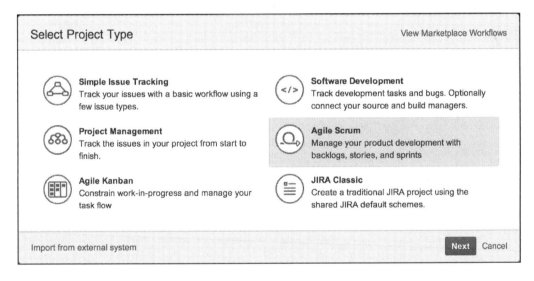

3. Enter your project's name and description, and click on the **Submit** button to create the new project.

 The Agile Scrum and Agile Kanban templates are present when you first install JIRA, but they are only usable after JIRA Agile is installed.

As we will see in later chapters, to use JIRA Agile, you do not have to use these templates. You can enable JIRA Agile and create agile boards for any existing projects. These templates are simply tools to help you get started quickly.

Summary

In this chapter, we looked at some of the basics of JIRA Agile, what it is, and what it is not. JIRA Agile is an add-on that lets you visualize your issues in a different way, and by leveraging many of the core features of JIRA, it keeps the learning curve low, especially for seasoned JIRA users.

Now that we have laid out the basics of JIRA Agile, we will start to explore how we can use it to run agile projects, starting with the Scrum methodology in the next chapter.

2
JIRA Agile for Scrum

Scrum is one of the agile methodologies supported by JIRA Agile. Unlike the old days, when a project manager would use either a spreadsheet or Microsoft project to keep track of the project progress, with JIRA Agile and Scrum, team participation is encouraged, to improve collaboration between different project stakeholders. In this chapter, we will look at how we can use JIRA Agile to unlock the power of Scrum.

By the end of the chapter, you will have learned about the following topics:

- An overview of Scrum
- Setting up a Scrum board
- Managing an issue backlog
- Estimating work and team velocities
- Running the Scrum sprint
- Tracking and reviewing sprint progress

Scrum

Unlike the traditional waterfall methodology where every task or project phase is sequential, Scrum prescribes the notion of iteration. At a high level, with Scrum, a project is broken up into a number of iterations called sprints. Each sprint is usually one or two weeks long; the project team completes a portion of the overall project, and the project is completed when all the sprints are finished. With this approach, the project team is able to do the following:

- Continuously deliver with each sprint, so feedback can be gathered early
- Accommodate changes during the project life cycle

- Identify issues early on rather than at the very end, which is costly
- Continuously improve the process with retrospective meetings at the end of each sprint

Roles in Scrum

In any Scrum team, there are three primary roles. Although each role has its own specific functions and responsibilities, you need all three to work together as a cohesive team in order to be successful at Scrum.

The product owner

The product owner is usually the product or project manager, who is responsible for owning the overall vision and the direction of the product that the team is working on. As the product owner, they are in charge of the features that will be added to the backlog list, the priority of each feature, and planning the delivery of these features through sprints. Essentially, the product owner is the person who makes sure that the team is delivering the most value for the stakeholders in each sprint.

The Scrum master

The Scrum master's job is to make sure that the team is running and using Scrum effectively and efficiently; so, they should be very knowledgeable and experienced with using Scrum. The Scrum master has the following two primary responsibilities:

- To coach and help everyone on the team to understand Scrum; this includes the product owner, delivery team, as well as external people that the project team interacts with. In the role of a coach, the Scrum master may help the product owner to understand and better manage the backlog and plan for sprints as well as explain the process with the delivery team.

- To improve the team's Scrum process by removing any obstacles in the way. Obstacles, also known as **impediments**, are anything that may block or negatively affect the team's adoption of Scrum. These can include things such as poorly-organized product backlog or the lack of support from other teams/management. It is the responsibility of the Scrum master to either directly remove these impediments or work with the team to find a solution.

Overall, the Scrum master is the advocate for Scrum, responsible for educating, facilitating, and helping people adopt and realize the advantages of using it.

The delivery team

The delivery team is primarily responsible for executing and delivering the final product. However, the team is also responsible for providing estimates on tasks and assisting the product owner to better plan sprints and delivery.

Ideally, the team should consist of cross-functional members required for the project, such as developers, testers, and business analysts. Since each sprint can be viewed as a mini project by itself, it is critical to have all the necessary resources available at all times, as tasks are being worked on and passed along the workflow.

Last but not least, the team is also responsible for retrospectively reviewing their performance at the end of each sprint, along with the product owner and Scrum master. This helps the team review what they have done and reveals how they can improve for the upcoming sprints.

Understanding the Scrum process

Now, we will give you a brief introduction to Scrum and an overview of the various roles that Scrum prescribes. Let's take a look at how a typical project is run with Scrum and some of the key activities.

First, we have the backlog, which is a one-dimensional list of the features and requirements that need to be implemented by the team. The item's backlogs are listed from top to bottom by priority. While the product owner is the person in charge of the backlog, defining the priority based on his vision, everyone in the team can contribute by adding new items to the backlog, discussing priorities, and estimating efforts required for implementation.

The team will then start planning their next immediate sprint. During this sprint planning meeting, the team will decide on the scope of the sprint. Usually, top priority items from the backlog will be included. The key here is that by the end of the sprint, the team should have produced a fully tested, potentially shippable product containing all the committed features.

During the sprint, the team will have daily Scrum meetings, usually at the start of each day, where every member of the team will give a quick overview of what they have done, plan to do, and any impediments. The goal is to make sure that everyone is on the same page, so meetings should be short and sweet.

At the end of the sprint, the team will have a sprint review meeting, where the team will present what they have produced to the stakeholder. During this meeting, new changes will often emerge as the product starts to take shape, and these changes will be added to the backlog, which the team will reprioritize before the next sprint commences.

Another meeting called the sprint retrospective meeting will also take place at the end of the sprint, where the team will come together to discuss what they have done right, what they have done wrong, and how they can improve.

Throughout this process, the Scrum master will act as the referee, where they will make sure all these activities are done correctly. For example, the Scrum master will guide the product owner and the team during the backlog and sprint planning meetings to make sure the items they have are scoped and described correctly. The Scrum master will also ensure that the meetings stay focused, productive, do not run overtime, and that the team members remain respectful without trying to talk over each other.

So, now you have seen some of the advantages of using Scrum, the different roles, as well as a simple Scrum process; let's see how we can use JIRA Agile to run projects with Scrum.

Creating a new Scrum board

The first step to start using JIRA Agile for Scrum is to create a Scrum board for your project. If you created your project by using the Agile Scrum project template, a Scrum board is automatically created for you along with the project.

However, if you want to create a board for existing projects, or if you want your board to span across multiple projects, you will need to create it separately. To create a new board, perform the following steps:

1. Click on the **Agile** menu item from the top navigation bar and select the **Manage Boards** option.
2. Click on the **Create board** button. This will bring up the **Create an Agile board** dialog.
3. Select the **Create a Scrum board** option, as shown in the following screenshot:

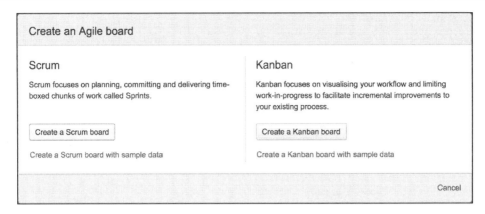

4. Select the way you want to create your board and click on the **Next** button. There are three options to choose from, as follows:

  ° **New project and a new board**: This is the same as creating a project using the Scrum Agile project template. A new project will be created along with a new Scrum board dedicated to the project.

  ° **Board from an existing project**: This option allows you to create a new board from your existing projects. The board will be dedicated to only one project.

  ° **Board from an existing Saved Filter**: This option allows you to create a board that can span across multiple projects with the use of a filter. So, in order to use this option, you will first have to create a filter that includes the projects and issues you need.

 If you have many issues in your project, you can also use filters to limit the number of issues to be included.

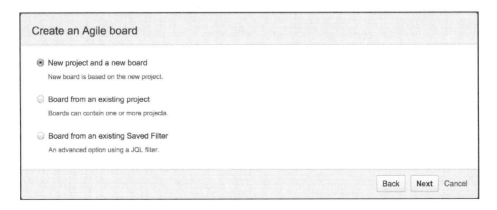

5. Fill in the required information for the board. Depending on the option you have selected, you will either need to provide the project details or select a filter to use. The following screenshot shows an example of how to create a board with a filter. Click on the **Create board** button to finish:

Understanding the Scrum board

The Scrum board is what you and your team will be using to plan and run your project. It is your backlog as well as your sprint activity board. A Scrum board has the following three major modes:

- **Backlog**: The **Backlog** mode is where you will plan your sprints, organize your backlog, and create issues
- **Active sprints**: The **Active sprints** mode is where your team will be working in a sprint
- **Reports**: The **Reports** mode is where you can track the progress of your sprint

The following screenshot shows a typical Scrum board in the **Backlog** mode. In the center of the page, you have the backlog, listing all the issues. You can drag them up and down to reorder their priorities. On the right-hand side, you have the issue details panel, which will be displayed when you click on an issue in the backlog:

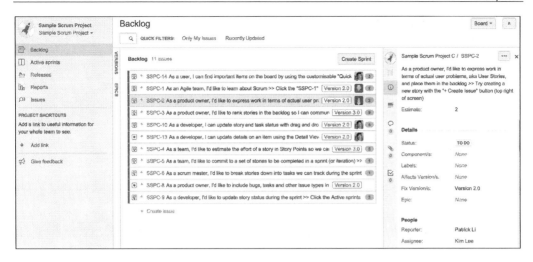

During the backlog planning meetings, the product owner and the team will use this **Backlog** mode to add new items to the backlog as well as decide on their priorities.

Creating new issues

When a Scrum board is first created, all the issues, if any (called user stories or stories for short), are placed in the backlog. During your sprint planning meetings, you can create more issues and add them to the backlog as you translate requirements into user stories. To create a new issue, perform the following steps:

1. Browse to your Scrum board.

2. Click on the **Create** button from the navigation bar at the top or press *C* on your keyboard. This will bring up the **Create Issue** dialog.

3. Select the type of issue (for example, **Story**) you want to create from the **Issue Type** field.

4. Provide additional information for the issue, such as **Summary** and **Description**.

5. Click on the **Create** button to create the issue, as shown in the following screenshot:

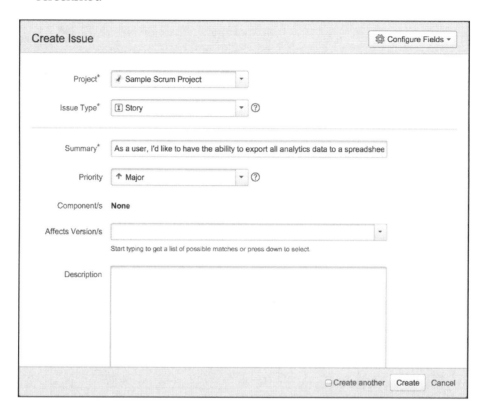

Once you have created the issue, it will be added to the backlog. You can then assign it to epics or version, and schedule it to be completed by adding it to sprints.

When creating and refining your user stories, you will want to break them down as much as possible, so that when it comes to deciding on the scope of a sprint, it will be much easier for the team to provide an estimate. One approach is by using the **INVEST** characteristics defined by Bill Wake:

*   **Independent**: It is preferable if each story can be done independently. While this is not always possible, independent tasks make implementation easier.
*   **Negotiable**: The developers and product owners need to work together so that both parties are fully aware of what the story entails.
*   **Valuable**: The story needs to provide value to the customer.
*   **Estimable**: If a story is too big or complicated for the development team to provide an estimate, then it needs to be broken down further.

- **Small**: Each story needs to be small, often addressing a single feature that will fit into a single sprint (roughly 2 weeks).

- **Testable**: The story needs to describe the expected end result so that after it is implemented, it can be verified.

Creating new epics

Epics are big user stories that describe major application features. They are then broken down into smaller, more manageable user stories. In JIRA Agile, epics are a convenient way to group similar user stories together.

To create a new epic from your Scrum board, perform the following steps:

1. Expand the **Epics** panel if it is hidden, by clicking on **EPICS** from the left-hand side panel.

2. Click on the **Create Epic** link from the **Epics** panel. The link will appear when you hover your mouse over the panel. This will bring up the **Create Epic** dialog, with the **Project** and **Issue Type** fields already preselected for you:

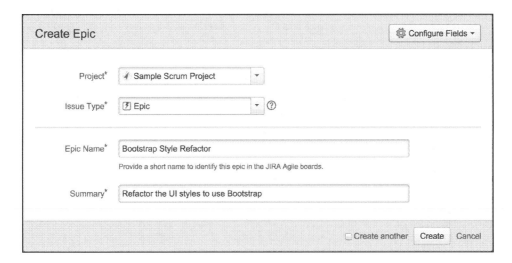

 You can also open the **Create issue** dialog, as show in the previous section, and select **Issue Type** as **Epic**.

3. Provide a name for the epic in the **Epic Name** field.

4. Provide a quick summary in the **Summary** field.

5. Click on the **Create** button.

Once you have created the epic, it will be added to the **Epics** panel.

 Epics do not show up as cards in sprints or in the backlog.

After you have created your epic, you can start adding issues under it. Doing this helps you organize issues that are related to the same functionality or feature. There are two ways in which you can add issues to an epic:

- By creating new issues directly in the epic, expanding the epic you want, and clicking on the **Create issue in epic** link

- By dragging existing issues into the epic, as shown in the following screenshot:

Estimating your work

Estimation is an art and is a big part of Scrum. Being able to estimate well as a team will directly impact how successful your sprints will be. When it comes to Scrum, estimation means velocity. In other words, it means how much work your team can deliver in a sprint. This is different from the traditional idea of measuring and estimating by man hours.

The concept of measuring velocity is to decouple estimation from time tracking. So, instead of estimating the work based on how many hours it will take to complete a story, which will inadvertently make people work long hours trying to keep the estimates accurate, it can be easily done by using an arbitrary number for measurement, which will help us avoid this pitfall.

A common approach is to use what are known as story points. Story points are used to measure the complexity or level of effort required to complete a story, not how long it will take to complete it. For example, a complex story may have eight story points, while a simpler story will have only two. This does not mean that the complex story will take 8 hours to complete. It is simply a way to measure its complexity in relation to others.

After you have estimated all your issues with story points, you need to figure out how many story points your team can deliver in a sprint. Of course, you will not know this for your first sprint, so you will have to estimate this again. Let's say your team is able to deliver 10 story points worth of work in a one-week sprint, then you can create sprints with any number of issues that add up to 10 story points. As your team starts working on the sprint, you will likely find that the estimate of 10 story points is too much or not enough, so you will need to adjust this for your second sprint. Remember that the goal here is not to get it right the first time but to continuously improve your estimates to a point where the team can consistently deliver the same amount of story points' worth of work, that is, your team's velocity. Once you accurately start predicting your team's velocity, it will become easier to manage the workload for each sprint.

Now that you know how estimates work in Scrum, let's look at how JIRA Agile lets you estimate work.

JIRA Agile provides several ways for you to estimate issues, and the most common approach is to use story points. Each story in your backlog has a field called **Estimate**, as shown in the following screenshot. To provide an estimate for the story, you just need to hover over the field, click on it, and enter the story point value:

You cannot set estimates once the issue is in active development, that is, the sprint that the issue belongs to is active.

Remember that the estimate value you provide here is arbitrary, as long as it can reflect the issues' complexity in relation to each other. Here are a few more points for estimation:

- Be consistent on how you estimate issues.
- Involve the team during estimation.
- If the estimates turn out to be incorrect, it is fine. The goal here is to improve and adjust.

Ranking and prioritizing your issues

During the planning session, it is important to rank your issues so that the list reflects their importance relative to each other. For those who are familiar with JIRA, there is a priority field, but since it allows you to have more than one issue sharing the same priority value, it becomes confusing when you have two issues both marked as critical.

JIRA Agile addresses this issue by letting you simply drag an issue up and down the list according to its importance, with the more important issues at the top and the less important issues at the bottom. This way, you end up with an easy-to-understand list.

Creating new versions

In a software development team, you will likely be using versions to plan your releases. Using versions allows you to plan and organize issues in your backlog and schedule when they will be completed. You can create multiple versions and plan your roadmap accordingly.

To create a new version, follow these steps:

1. Expand the **Versions** panel if it is hidden, by clicking on **VERSIONS** from the left-hand side panel.

2. Click on the **Create Version** link from the **Versions** panel. The link will appear when you hover your mouse over the panel. This will bring up the **Create Version** dialog with the **Project** field preselected for you, as shown in the following screenshot:

3. Provide a name for the version in the **Name** field.
4. You can also specify the start and release dates for the version. These fields are optional, and you can change them later.
5. Click on the **Create** button.

Once the version is created, it will be added to the **Versions** panel. Just like epics, you can add issues to a version by dragging and dropping the issue over onto the target version. In Scrum, a version can span across many sprints. Clicking on a version will display the issues that are part of the version. As shown in the following screenshot, **Version 2.0** spans across three sprints:

Planning sprints

The sprint planning meeting is where the project team comes together at the start of each sprint and decides what they should focus and work on next. With JIRA Agile, you will be using the **Backlog** mode of your board to create and plan the new sprint's scope.

Now we illustrate some of the key components during sprint planning:

- **Backlog**: This includes all the issues that are not in any sprint yet. In other words, it includes the issues that are not yet scheduled for completion. For a new board, all existing issues will be placed in the backlog.

- **Sprints**: These are displayed above the backlog. You can have multiple sprints and plan ahead.

- **Issue details**: This is the panel on your right-hand side. It displays details of the issue you are clicking on.

- **Epics**: This is one of the panels on your left-hand side. It displays all the epics you have.

- **Versions**: This is the other panel on your left-hand side. It displays all the versions you have.

The highlighted area in the following screenshot is the new sprint, and the issues inside the sprint are what the team has committed to deliver at the end of the sprint:

Starting a sprint

Once all the epics and issues have been created, it is time to start preparing a sprint. The first step is to create a new sprint by clicking on the **Create Sprint** button.

There are two ways to add issues to a sprint:

- By dragging the issues you want from backlog and dropping them into the sprint

- By dragging the sprint footer down, to include all the issues you want to be part of the sprint

You can create multiple sprints and plan beyond the current one by filling each sprint with issues from your backlog.

Once you have all the issues you want in the sprint, click on the **Start Sprint** link. As shown in the following screenshot, you will be asked to set the start and end dates of the sprint. By default, JIRA Agile will automatically set the start date to the current date, and the end date to one week after that. You can change these dates, of course. The general best practices include the following:

- Keeping your sprints short, usually 1 or 2 weeks long.
- Keeping the length of your sprints consistent; this way, you will be able to accurately predict your team's velocity:

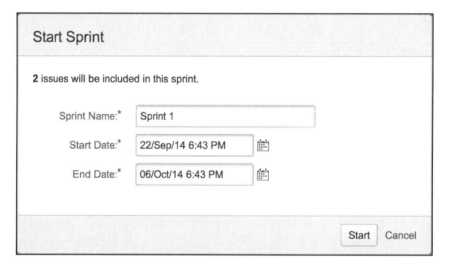

Once you have started your sprint, you will be taken to the active sprints mode for the board.

Note that for you to start a sprint, you have to take following things into consideration:

- There must be no sprint already active. You can only have one active sprint per board at any time. There is an option that allows you to run parallel sprints, which we will talk about in *Chapter 5, JIRA Agile – Advanced*.
- You must have the **Administer Projects** permission for all projects included in the board.

Working on a sprint

You will enter the active sprint mode once you have started a sprint; all the issues that are part of the sprint will be displayed. In the active sprint mode, the board will be divided into two major sections.

The left section will contain all the issues in the current sprint. You will notice that it is divided into several columns. These columns represent the various states or statuses that an issue can be in, and they should reflect your team's workflow. By default, there are three columns:

- **To Do**: The issue is waiting to start
- **In Progress**: The issue is currently being worked on
- **Done**: The issue has been completed

As we will see in the next chapter, you can customize these columns by mapping them to JIRA workflow statuses.

If you are using epics to organize your issues, this section will also be divided into several horizontal swimlanes. Swimlanes help you group similar issues together on the board. Swimlanes group issues by criteria, such as assignee, story, or epic. By default, swimlanes are grouped by stories, so subtasks for the same story will all be placed in one swimlane.

So, you can see that columns group issues by statuses, while swimlanes group issues by similarity. As shown in the following screenshot, we have three columns and two swimlanes:

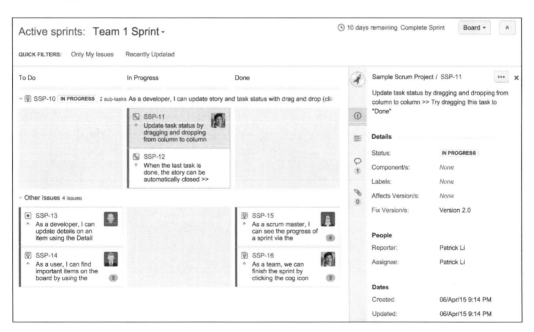

The section on the right-hand side displays the currently selected issue's details, such as its summary and description, comments, and attachments.

In a typical scenario, at the start of a sprint, all the issues will be in the left-most **To Do** column. During the daily Scrum meetings, team members will review the current status of the board and decide what to focus on for the day. For example, each member of the team may take on an issue and move it to the **In Progress** column by simply dragging and dropping the issue cards into the column. Once they have finished working on the issues, they can drag them into the **Done** column. The team will continue this cycle throughout the sprint until all the issues are completed:

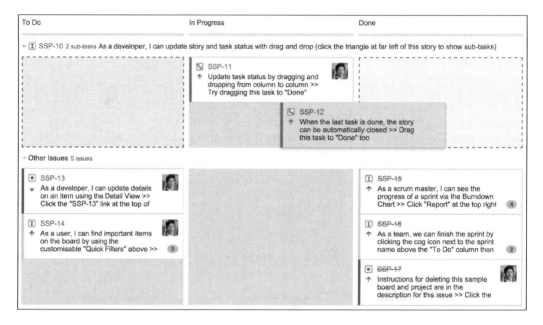

During the sprint, the Scrum master as well as the product owner will need to make sure not to interrupt the team unless it is urgent. The Scrum master should also assist with removing impediments that are preventing team members from completing their assigned tasks.

The product owner should also ensure that no additional stories are added to the sprint, and any new feature requests are added to the backlog for future sprints instead. JIRA Agile will alert you if you try to add a new issue to the currently active sprint.

Completing a sprint

On the day the sprint ends, you will need to complete the sprint by performing the following steps:

1. Go to your Scrum board and click on **Active sprints**.

2. Click on the **Complete Sprint** link. This will bring up the **Complete Sprint** dialog, summarizing the current status of the sprint. As shown in the following screenshot, we have a total of six issues in this sprint. Three issues are completed and three are not:

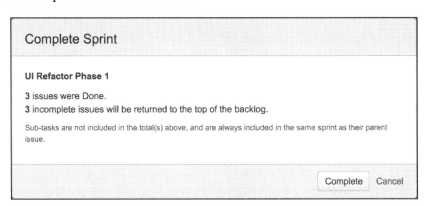

3. Click on the **Complete** button to complete the sprint.

When you complete a sprint, any unfinished issues will be automatically moved back to the top of the backlog. Sometimes, it might be tempting to extend your sprint if you only have one or two issues outstanding, but you should not do this. Remember that the goal here is not to make your estimates appear accurate by extending sprints or to force your team to work harder in order to complete everything. You want to get to a point where the team is consistently completing the same amount of work in each sprint. If you have leftovers from a sprint, it means that your team's velocity should be lowered. Therefore, for the next sprint, you should plan to include less work.

Reporting a sprint's progress

As your team busily works through the issues in the sprint, you need to have a way to track the progress. JIRA Agile provides a number of useful reports via the **Report** mode. You can access the **Report** mode anytime during the sprint. These reports are also very useful during sprint retrospective meetings, as they provide detailed insights on how the sprint progressed.

The sprint report

The sprint report gives you a quick snapshot of how the sprint is tracking. It includes a burndown chart (see the next section) and a summary table that lists all the issues in the sprint and their statuses, as shown here:

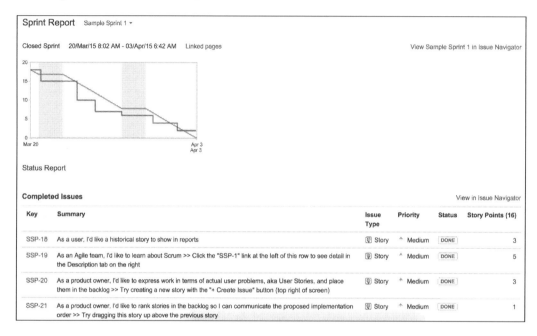

As shown in the preceding sprint report, we have completed four issues in the sprint. One issue was not completed and was placed back in the backlog.

The burndown chart

The burndown chart shows you a graphical representation of the estimated or ideal work left versus actual progress. The gray line acts as a guideline of the projected progress of the project, and the red line is the actual progress. In an ideal world, both lines should be as close to each other as possible, as the sprint progresses each day:

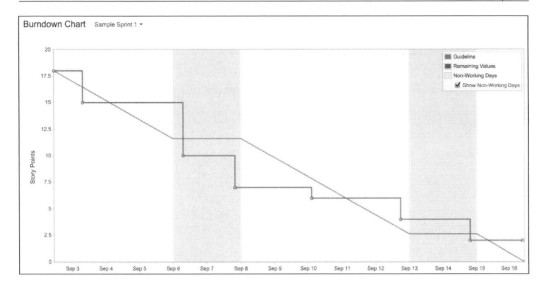

The velocity chart

The velocity chart shows you the amount of work originally committed to the sprint (the gray bar) versus the actual amount of work completed (the green bar), based on how you decide to estimate, such as in the case of story points.

The chart will include past sprints, so you can get an idea of the trend and be able to predict the team's velocity. As shown in the following screenshot, from sprint 1 to 3, we have over-committed the amount of work, and for sprint 4, we have completed all our committed work. So, one way to work out your team's velocity is to calculate the average based on the **Completed** column, and this should give you an indication of your team's true velocity. Of course, this requires:

- That your sprints stay consistent in duration
- That your team members stay consistent
- That your estimation stays consistent

As your team starts using Scrum, you can expect to see improvements to the team's velocity, as you continuously refine your process. Over time, you will get to a point where the team's velocity becomes consistent and can be used as a reliable indicator for work estimation. This will allow you to avoid over and under committing on work delivery, as shown in the following velocity chart:

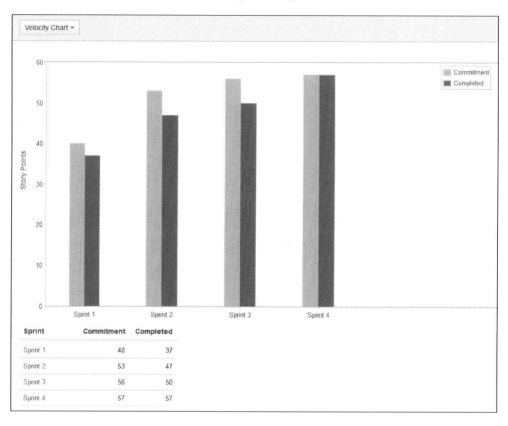

Sprint	Commitment	Completed
Sprint 1	40	37
Sprint 2	53	47
Sprint 3	56	50
Sprint 4	57	57

Summary

In this chapter, we looked at how to use JIRA Agile for Scrum. We looked at the Scrum board and how you can use it to organize your issue backlog, plan and run your sprint, and review and track its progress with reports and charts. Remember that the keys for a successfully running sprint are consistency, review, and continuous improvement. It is fine if you find your estimates are incorrect, especially for the first few sprints; just make sure that you review, adjust, and improve.

Now that you have seen how to use a Scrum board, in the next chapter, we will dive into the more advanced features of JIRA Agile and how you can customize your Scrum board to better suite your team's workflow.

3
Customizing the Scrum Board

In the previous chapter, we looked at how to use JIRA Agile for the Scrum agile methodology. JIRA Agile comes with a set of tools to support Scrum, and sensible defaults to get you up and running quickly. However, you will often need to customize what comes out of the box by default, in order to better suit your needs. In this chapter, we will go over some of the most important options JIRA Agile provides, so it can better adapt to the way you need to run Scrum.

By the end of the chapter, you will have learned to:

- Manage your Scrum board's configuration
- Control what issues are to be included on your board
- Customize your Scrum board's column layouts
- Use swimlanes to group your issues
- Filter issues on your Scrum board with quick filters

Managing your board

When you first create a Scrum board using JIRA Agile's built-in templates, as outlined in *Chapter 2, JIRA Agile for Scrum*, the board is created with a set of default settings. Now, you as the board's administrator can go and customize these. To customize a board, perform the following steps:

1. Go to the Scrum board you want to customize.
2. Click on the **Board** drop-down menu and select the **Configure** option.

3.   Select **General** from the left navigation:

You can update the configuration options by first hovering over the field value, and then clicking on the edit (pencil) icon. The following table provides a summary of the configuration fields:

Field	Description
Board Name	Name for the agile board.
Administrators	Users who can configure the agile board's settings. You can add more administrators by either selecting the users directly, or by selecting a group.
Saved Filter	This controls what issues will be included on the agile board. If you have created your board using the agile templates, then the filter here is automatically created for you to include all issues in the project. You can select a different filter to use, or click on the **Edit Filter Query** link to change the current filter.
Shares	This controls who will have access to the filter. In practice, the filter should be shared with the same users who have access to the board.
Filter Query	This shows you the actual filter query used by **Saved Filter**.
Ranking	This shows if ranking is currently enabled. You need to have ranking enabled to rank issues and create sprints.

Enabling ranking

Ranking allows you to prioritize your issues by dragging and dropping them into your backlog and sprints. The higher an issue is, the more important it is. If ranking is disabled, you will get an error message similar to `Ranking is disabled, as the Filter Query for this board is not ordered by Rank`, when you try to drag your issues in the **Plan** mode.

If you have created your agile board by using the agile templates with either the new project or existing project option, then ranking will be enabled by default. However, if it is disabled for some reason, you can enable ranking by following the next few steps:

1. Go to the Scrum board you want to customize.
2. Click on the **Board** drop-down menu and select the **Configure** option.
3. Select **General** from the left navigation.
4. Click on the **Add Rank** button at the bottom to enable ranking:

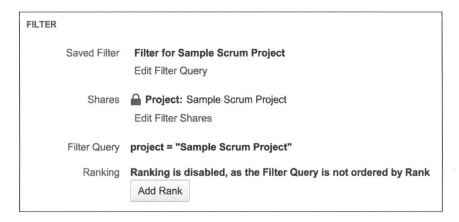

After you have enabled ranking, you will notice that your **Filter Query** value is automatically updated. So in the preceding screenshot, the query `project = "Sample Scrum Project"` will be changed to `project = "Sample Scrum Project" ORDER BY Rank ASC`. Make sure you do not remove the `ORDER BY Rank ASC` part of the query, as that is the snippet that enables ranking for your query and board.

The active sprint mode

The active sprint mode for a Scrum board acts as the white board where all your story cards are placed. There are some key components that make up the board, namely the columns and swimlanes.

- **Columns**: The vertical columns are used to represent the state of a story card
- **Swimlanes**: The horizontal rows that help you to better categorize your story cards on the board

In the following sections, we will take a deeper look into these two components and how you, as the board administrator, can customize them to get the most out of your board.

Working with columns

Columns represent the statuses an issue can be in. On a simple board, as shown in the following screenshot, we have three columns, and they are each mapped to an issue status:

- **To Do**: Issues that are waiting in queue to be worked on are mapped to the **To Do** workflow status
- **In Progress**: Issues that are currently being worked on are mapped to the **In Progress** workflow status
- **Done**: Issues that are completed are mapped to the Done workflow status:

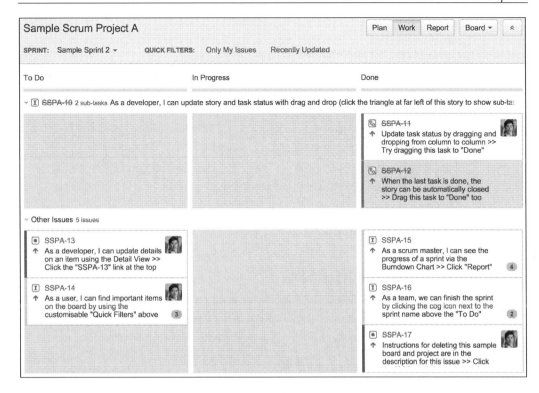

This is a very simple setup where issues only have three steps from start to finish. Often, you will have an existing workflow that is more complex than this.

JIRA Agile and workflows

Before we get into customizing columns, we first need to take a quick look at workflows in relation to JIRA Agile. As you may already know, JIRA uses workflows to move an issue from one status to the next. JIRA Agile also leverages this feature by mapping its columns to workflow statuses.

Since workflows in JIRA can often get very complicated, it sometimes makes it difficult to use the traditional JIRA workflows in an agile environment, so JIRA Agile introduced what is known as **Agile Simplified Workflow**.

Agile Simplified Workflow refers to workflows that are managed directly from within JIRA Agile, and are simplified and streamlined for agile usage. This allows you to:

- Maintain your workflow from your agile board, managed as board columns
- Move issues freely from one status (column) to another without restrictions from workflow conditions and validators
- Not have intermediate screens when you move issues between statuses, making it much easier to move cards (issues) on your boards
- Automatically set resolution values (as per your definition) when issues are moved to appropriate statuses (columns)

If you have created your agile board by using the built-in agile templates, then you are most likely using Agile Simplified Workflow.

Creating new columns

If you are the board administrator, you can customize the board's columns to better reflect your workflow:

1. Navigate to the Scrum board that you want to customize.
2. Click on the **Board** drop-down menu and select the **Configure** option.
3. Select **Columns** from the left navigation.

From the **Column management** page, you can customize the following options:

- **Columns**: You can add, remove, and rename columns.
- **Column Layout**: You can rearrange the order of columns.
- **Issue Status Mapping**: You can map columns to issue statuses. For each column, you can have one or more issue statuses mapped to it.
- **Column Constraint**: You can add constraints to columns, limiting how many issues can be in a status at any given time.

Let's start with creating new columns. There are two ways new columns can be created and mapped to issue statuses, depending on whether you are using Agile Simplified Workflow or not. You can determine if you are using the simplified workflow by looking at the **Simplified Workflow** field, and seeing if it says **Using Agile Simplified Workflow**, as shown in the following screenshot:

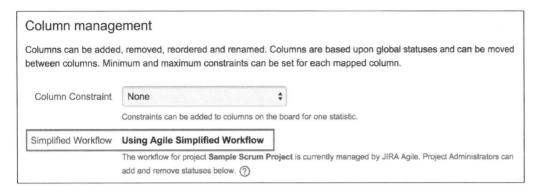

For a new column to be usable, it needs to have at least one status mapped. If you are using Agile Simplified Workflow, this is a very straightforward process. The Agile Simplified Workflow takes care of this for you, so you don't have to worry about manual column status mapping. It is recommended to use Agile Simplified Workflow where possible. To add a new column, perform the following steps:

1. Click on the **Add column** button. A new column will be added to the list in the second-last position.

2. Enter a name for the new column. A new issue status will also be created with the same name, and mapped to the new column.

If you are not using the Agile Simplified Workflow, you will need to perform the following steps:

1. Create the new column as outlined in the preceding list.

2. Create new workflow statuses to be mapped to the new column, and add the statuses used by the workflow.

3. Manually drag and drop the statuses into the new column, as shown in the following screenshot:

You can also map additional statuses to columns by dragging the status you want to map from under the **Unmapped Statuses** section, and dropping them into the target column. Once you have mapped at least one status to the new column, it will be displayed on the board in active sprint mode.

It is recommended to have one column per workflow status to keep the flow logical and simple. However, you can have multiple statuses mapped to one column, as shown in the preceding screenshot, we have both **Done** and **Fixed** statuses mapped to the **Done** column. You will usually find the need to do this if you are creating a Scrum board for an existing project with a workflow in place, or you have a complex workflow that cannot be mapped to columns on the board one-to-one.

When you map multiple statuses to a column, such as the **Done** column in our example, and move an issue into the column, you will be able to select the appropriate status, as shown in the following screenshot:

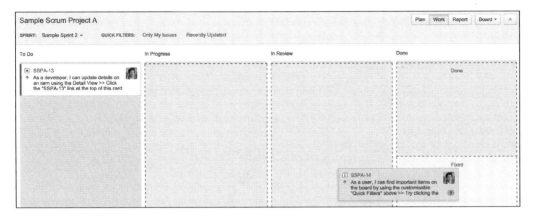

When using Agile Simplified Workflow, you will see a checkbox option called **Set resolution** in the mapped workflow status. If you check this option, when an issue is moved into the corresponding column, it will be automatically assigned the resolution value of **Done**. JIRA Agile makes use of resolution value to determine if an issue has been completed, so it is important to assign a value for the status/column that represents the end of the workflow.

 If you are not using the Agile Simplified Workflow, this option is not available; resolution must be set using a workflow transition screen.

Setting up column layout

Once you have created all your new columns and mapped them to workflow statuses, you can re-arrange the column layout by dragging and dropping the columns left and right to their desired locations, as shown in the following screenshot. The order of your column should reflect your workflow, starting from the left and moving right, so it visually represents the logical flow of an issue through the work process:

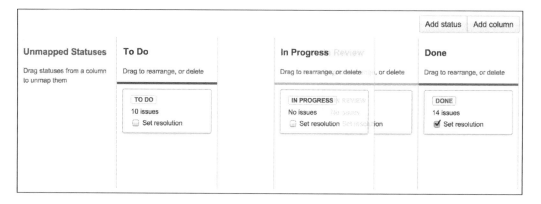

As we will see in *Chapter 5, JIRA Agile – Advanced*, you will be able to export your issues from your board onto a physical board and import them back in, as long as the column layout of your JIRA Agile board is the same as your physical board.

Setting up column constraint

JIRA Agile lets you specify constraints for your columns, to limit the number of issues that can be in a column at any given time. For example, you can set a constraint that there should be a minimum of three and no more than five issues in the In Progress column, as shown in the following screenshot:

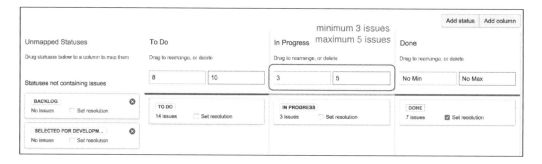

Setting column constraints is not a normal practice for pure Scrum; it is used most commonly in Kanban; refer to *Chapter 4, JIRA Agile for Kanban*. However, people have found that some of the benefits of Kanban, such as using column constraints to identify problems in the workflow and improve the process, results in what is called **Scrum-ban**. To set up column constraints:

1. Select how you would like to count the number of issues in the **Column Constraint** field.

2. Enter the minimum and/or maximum values for the column you want to place a constraint on. You can have either a minimum or maximum, or both.

Once you have placed constraints on a column, if it is violated, the column will be highlighted. As shown in the following screenshot, the **In Progress** column has a maximum constraint of four issues, but we have five, so it is highlighted in red. The **In Review** column has a minimum constraint of two issues, but we have one, so it is highlighted in yellow:

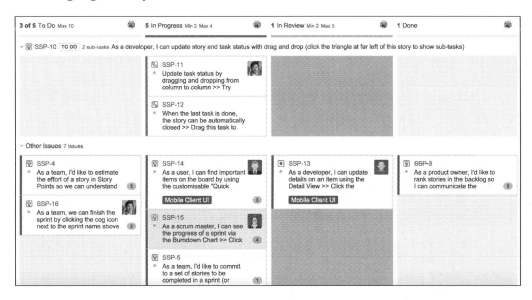

Column constraints do not prevent you from violating the limits. They simply help to flag areas where there might be a problem. Setting the limits for your columns can be tricky, especially when you are just getting started. You should start with your "gut feeling" and run a few sprints, and refine the limits as you and your team get a better feel for the workflow. One way to get started is to base your limits on the number of people you have on your team. For example, if you have five developers, then your maximum limit for your **In Progress** columns (assuming it means development) should be no more than five, as it is not logical to have five people working on six issues at the same time.

So, if we look at the example in the preceding screenshot, we are over the maximum limit for the **In Progress** column. This could mean that the team, especially the developers, has overcommitted on their tasks; someone might have decided to work on two tasks in parallel. This is causing a bottleneck and issues are not being completed quick enough to move to the **In Review** column, causing a minimum limit violation, where you have reviewers waiting around for work. This data can be very useful in your sprint retrospective meetings, to review the problem and refine the process.

So as you can see, setting column constraints is situational and is based on your team's composition, as well as their abilities. As things change, you will need to change your limits accordingly. Remember, the goal here is to measure, identify, and improve.

Working with swimlanes

Swimlanes are the horizontal counterparts to columns on a board. Unlike columns, which are always mapped to issue statuses, you can base your swimlanes on several criteria:

- **Queries**: These are JIRA search queries constructed with JQL. With this option, each swimlane will only show results from its own query. For example, you can create a query for each priority value, so you can group your issues based on their importance.

- **Stories**: Each swimlane will be mapped to a story. All sub-tasks that fall under the story will be displayed in the swimlane.

- **Assignees**: Each swimlane will be mapped based on the issue's assignee.

- **Epics**: Each swimlane will be mapped to an epic. All issues that fall under the epic will be displayed in the swimlane.

Using swimlanes is a great way to group and categorize your issues on your Scrum board. For example, with the **Assignees** option, you can easily get an idea of each team member's workload by just looking at the board. The following screenshot shows a Scrum board with three swimlanes based on issue priority, by using the queries option:

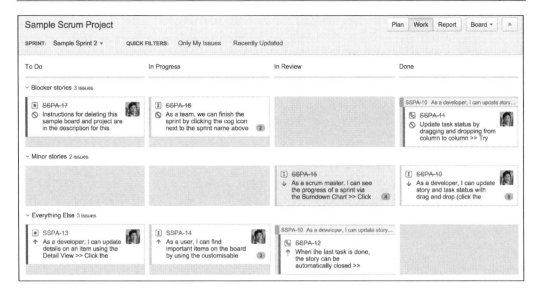

Setting up swimlanes

If you are the board administrator, you can customize the board's swimlanes to better organize your story cards:

1. Navigate to the Scrum board you want to customize.

2. Click on the **Board** drop-down menu and select the **Configure** option.

3. Select **Swimlane** from the left navigation.

4. Choose the criteria you want to base your swimlanes on, from the **Base Swimlanes on** field.

5. If you choose to base your swimlanes on **Queries**, you will need to enter the name for each swimlane and its corresponding JQL query, as shown in the following screenshot:

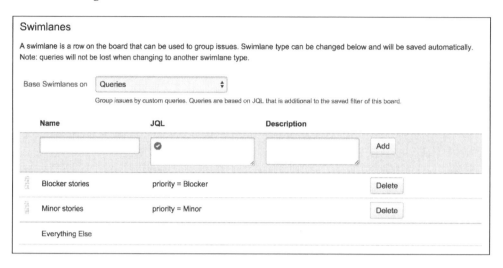

Using quick filters

When you have many issues on your board, sometimes you would want to narrow them down and focus on issues that fit specific criteria, such as bugs or new stories. By using quick filters, we can remove the unnecessary "noise" by filtering out all the issues that do not fit the criteria, letting you focus on the issues to care about. Have a look at the following screenshot:

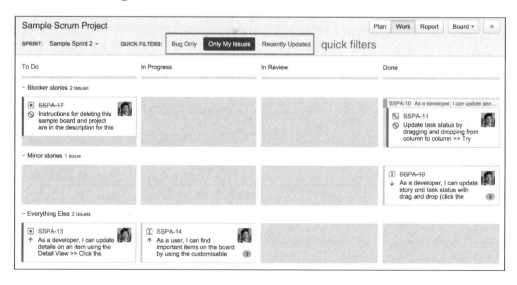

You can think of quick filters as additional views for your Scrum board. For example, the preceding screenshot shows three quick filters for your Scrum board, **Bug Only**, **Only My Issues**, and **Recently Updated**. By using the **Bug Only** quick filter, you can get a view of your board showing only bug issues. You can toggle a quick filter on and off by clicking on it. When turned on, it will be highlighted in blue, and update the board with only issues that fit the filter's criteria. Clicking on the filter again will un-apply it. You can have more than one quick filter applied to a board at the same time, and only issues that fit both the filters' criteria will be shown.

Creating new quick filters

All agile boards come with two default quick filters:

- **Only My Issues**: This displays issues that are assigned to the currently logged in user
- **Recently Updated**: This displays issues that have been updated in the last 24 hours

If you are the board administrator, you can create new quick filters for your board to help you and your team to better visualize your issues. To do this, perform the following steps:

1. Navigate to the Scrum board that you want to customize.
2. Click on the **Board** drop-down menu and select the **Configure** option.
3. Select **Quick Filters** from the left navigation.
4. Enter a name for the filter in the **Name** field. The name entered here will be displayed on the agile board.
5. Enter the search query for the filter in the **JQL** field, as shown in the following screenshot.
6. Click on the **Add** button to create the new filter.

Once created, the new quick filter will be available to everyone using the Scrum board:

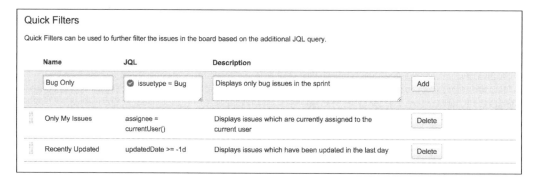

In our example, as shown in the preceding screenshot, the JQL query `issuetype =
Bug` means to include issues that have the value `Bug` for their issue type field. JQL is
a feature of JIRA that JIRA Agile leverages, and you can find more details about it at:
`https://confluence.atlassian.com/display/JIRA/Advanced+Searching`

Summary

In this chapter, we looked at how to customize a Scrum board in JIRA Agile. Some
of the important points we have covered include customizing the board's columns,
mapping Scrum board columns to JIRA workflow statuses, and using swimlanes to
group similar issues to better categorize our issues.

Now that we have covered using JIRA Agile for Scrum, we will take a look at how
to use it for another popular agile methodology, that is, Kanban.

4
JIRA Agile for Kanban

In the last two chapters, we have looked at how to use JIRA Agile for the Scrum Agile methodology. JIRA Agile also supports another agile methodology called Kanban, which many agile teams have chosen to use instead of Scrum. In this chapter, we will look at how to use JIRA Agile for Kanban.

By the end of the chapter, you will have learned to:

- Visualize workflow with Kanban
- Work on issues the Kanban way
- Customize your Kanban board
- Create reports and charts for improvements

Kanban

Kanban is the other agile methodology that is supported by JIRA Agile. Unlike Scrum which was introduced in *Chapter 2, JIRA Agile for Scrum*, which revolves around the notion of running your project in planned iterations called sprints, Kanban does not run in iterations, or rather, usage of iteration is optional with Kanban.

In a nutshell, Kanban has the following three concepts:

- **Visualize workflow**: This breaks down your tasks (issues) and puts them on the board. You need to organize your board so that each column represents a status in our overall workflow, ordered from left (start) to right (finish).

- **Limit work in progress (WIP)**: This sets minimum and maximum limits for how many tasks can be in any given workflow status.

- **Measure the lead time**: This calculates the average time required to complete one task, keeping it as low and predictable as possible.

Understanding the Kanban board

For those that are familiar with the Scrum board in JIRA Agile, the Kanban board will look very similar to the work mode of the Scrum board, with only a few differences:

- There is no backlog, or rather the first column on your board is your backlog

- There are no active sprints or sprint planning

- Some of the columns may have a minimum and maximum number, which appears next to the column name

- Some of the columns may be highlighted in red or yellow, as shown in the following screenshot, where the **In Progress** column is highlighted in red:

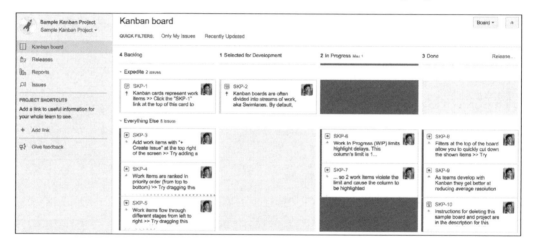

So, let's take a closer look at the Kanban board and see why we have these differences. First of all, as explained in the earlier section, Kanban does not use discrete time periods such as iterations to plan work in advance. Instead, work is being done constantly, going from the backlog to the finish line to be released. Therefore, the Kanban board does not have separate views for the backlog (or **Plan** mode in older versions of JIRA Agile) and the current active sprints (or **Work** mode), everything is combined into this single Kanban board view, which shows you everything in your backlog and the current progress as your team works through them.

Creating a new Kanban board

JIRA Agile provides a simple-to-follow wizard to help you create new Kanban boards. All you need to do is choose if you want to create a board from scratch, or from an existing project or filter, and follow the steps.

To create a new Kanban board, perform the following steps:

1. Click on the **Agile** menu from the top navigation bar and select the **Manage Boards** option.

2. Click on the **Create board** button. This will bring up the **Create an Agile board** dialog.

3. Select the **Create a Kanban board** option:

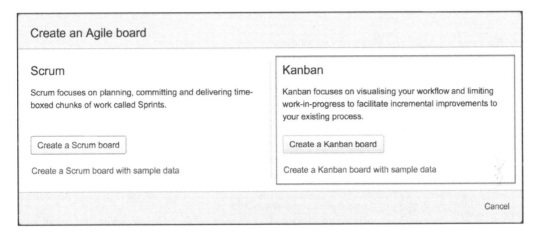

4. Select how you want to create your board and click on the **Next** button. There are three options to choose from to create your board. These options are explained as follows:

   ° **New project and a new board**: This is the same as creating a project using the Scrum Agile project template. A new project will be created along with a new Kanban board dedicated to the project.

   ° **Board from an existing project**: This option allows you to create a new board from your existing projects. The board will be dedicated to only one project.

   ° **Board from an existing Saved Filter**: This option allows you to create a board that can span across multiple projects with the use of a filter. So, to use this option, you will first have to create a filter that includes the projects and issues you need.

You can also use filters to limit the number of issues to be included, if you have many issues in your project.

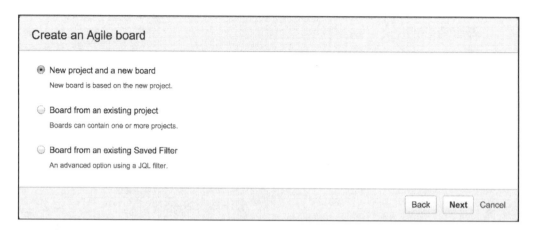

5. Fill in the required information for the board. Depending on the option you have selected, you will either need to provide the project details or select a filter to use. The following screenshot shows an example of creating a board with a filter. Click on the **Create board** button to finish:

Customizing your Kanban board

After you have created your Kanban board, you will need to customize it based on your workflow process and your team's capacity. Some of the key customizations include:

- Modeling your board columns to mimic your workflow
- Setting minimum and maximum constraints for your workflow status so as to control the work in progress
- Controlling what issues will be included and displayed on the board
- Categorizing issues on the Kanban board in swimlanes
- Creating custom filtered views with quick filters

Visualizing workflows with Kanban

One of the core concepts of Kanban is to visualize the team's workflow to better understand what the team is currently working on, what the workload is like, and where in the workflow a given task is.

In JIRA Agile, workflow statuses are represented as columns on the Kanban board, and you can customize your Kanban board's columns to closely mimic your actual workflow. To customize your Kanban board's columns, perform the following steps:

1. Go to the Kanban board you want to customize.
2. Click on the **Board** dropdown menu and select the **Configure** option.
3. Select **Columns** from the left navigation.
4. Click on the **Add column** button.
5. Enter a name for the new column and select a category for it. Generally speaking, if the column represents the start of the workflow, then it should be **To Do**. If it represents the end, then it should be **Done**. Otherwise, use **In Progress**.

6. Click on the **Add** button to create the new column:

Once you have created the new column, it will be added as the second last column on the list. You can rearrange that by dragging it left or right on the list, so it is in the correct position in your workflow.

Generally speaking, your board should reflect how work progresses through your workflow, so you should have a column for each major step that members of your team will be working on. For example, if you have these three steps in your workflow, **In Development**, **Development Completed**, and **In Testing**, you should have two columns, one for **In Development** and one for **In Testing**. The reason why you should not have a column for **Development Completed** is because nobody will be working on the issues that are in the step.

Setting up column constraints

As stated earlier, one of the key differences between Scrum and Kanban is that Scrum limits the amount of work per iteration, and Kanban limits the amount of work per workflow status. To set up column constraints, perform the following steps:

1. Go to the Kanban board you want to customize.
2. Click on the **Board** dropdown menu and select the **Configure** option.
3. Select **Columns** from the left navigation.

4. Choose how you want column constraint to be calculated from the **Column Constraint** field. If you select the **None** option, column constraint will not be applied to this board.

5. Set the minimum and maximum constraint value for the status in its corresponding columns. For example, as shown in the following screenshot, for the **Selected for Development** column, the team should have a minimum of five issues, and no more than ten issues in the status:

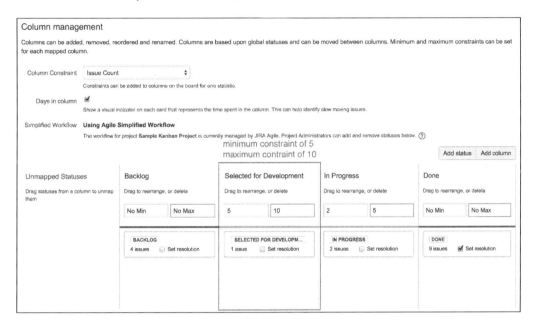

Once you have set the minimum and maximum constraints for workflow statuses, the Kanban board will let you know if those constraints are violated. For example, as shown in the following screenshot, we only have one issue in the **Selected for Development** status, which has a minimum constraint of 5 issues, so the column is highlighted in yellow. We also have six issues in the **In Progress** status, which has a maximum constraint of five issues, so the column is highlighted in red:

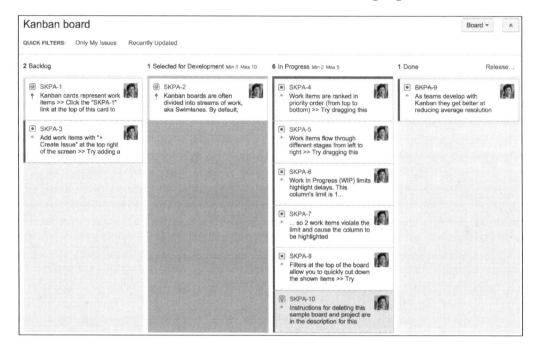

When you start seeing these constraint violations, it means the team should start reassessing the current workload.

Controlling what issues to show on the board

For Kanban board, there are two queries used to determine what issues will be displayed:

- **Saved Filter**: The saved filter includes issues that will be displayed on the Kanban board. The **Filter Query** field shows the JQL query of the saved filter. Depending on how the board is created, the saved filter will be either automatically created or selected from an existing filter list.

- **Kanban board sub-filter**: The sub-filter determines which issues from the saved filter will be considered unreleased. As we will see in the later section, *Releasing a version in Kanban*, once an issue is released as part of a new version, it is removed from the board.

As shown in the following screenshot, **Sample Kanban Board** is using the **Filter for Sample Kanban Project** saved filter with the JQL query of `project = "Sample Kanban Project" ORDER BY Rank ASC`. This means that all issues created in **Sample Kanban Project** will be shown on the board. It is also using the JQL query of `fixVersion in unreleasedVersions() OR fixVersion is EMPTY`, which means issues that have an unreleased version as their fix versions, or do not have a value for the field, will be considered unreleased and displayed on the board:

General and filter

The Board filter determines which issues appear on the board. It can be based on one or more projects, or custom JQL depending on your needs.

General

Board name	**Sample Kanban Project**
Administrators	**Patrick Li (patrick)**

Filter

Saved Filter	**Filter for Sample Kanban Project** Edit Filter Query
Shares	🔒 **Project:** Sample Kanban Project Edit Filter Shares
Filter Query	**project = SKP ORDER BY Rank ASC**
Ranking	**Using Rank**
Kanban board sub-filter	**fixVersion in unreleasedVersions() OR fixVersion is EMPTY** Further filtering of issues for unreleased work.

You can change both the saved filter and sub-filter used for your board. If you want to simply use a different saved filter for another filter you have, perform the following steps:

1. Hover over and click on the saved filter's name. You will see it change to a select list.

2. Select the new saved filter from the list. If you do not see the filter you want, you can type in the filter's name and search for it. Note that you can only see and select filters that you have access to.

You can also change the JQL query of the saved filter currently in use:

1. Click on the **Edit Filter Query** link under **Saved Filter**. This will bring you to **Issue Navigator**, the interface where you create and edit filters in JIRA, as shown in the following screenshot:

2. Update your search filter criteria via the UI controls if you are in the **Basic** mode, or the JQL query directly if you are in the **Advanced** mode.

3. Click on the **Save** button at the top to update your filter.

As shown in the preceding example, we changed our filter's query to `project = "Sample Kanban Project"` and `issuetype in (Bug, Story, Task) ORDER BY Rank ASC`, which limits the issues to types of bugs, stories, and tasks only.

To update the board's sub-filter to customize how unreleased issues are determined, here are the steps:

1. Hover over and click on the Kanban board sub-filter's content. You will see it change to an editable text box as shown in the following screenshot.

2. Enter the new JQL query and click on the **Update** button, as follows:

As shown in the preceding example, we have changed the sub-filter's query to `fixVersion in unreleasedVersions() OR fixVersion is EMPTY or resolution is EMPTY`, to also include a check for issues that do not have a value for the **Resolution** field.

Organizing your Kanban board with swimlanes

A swimlane is a useful way to group and organize your issues on your Kanban board. For example, you can use swimlanes to represent priority, and divide issues based on owners or types.

By default, when you first create a new Kanban board, you will have two swimlanes, but you can also create your own custom ones. For example, as shown in the following screenshot, we have three swimlanes: the **Expedite** and the **Everything Else** swimlanes are created along with your board, and the **Bugs** swimlane in the middle is a custom swimlane we have added:

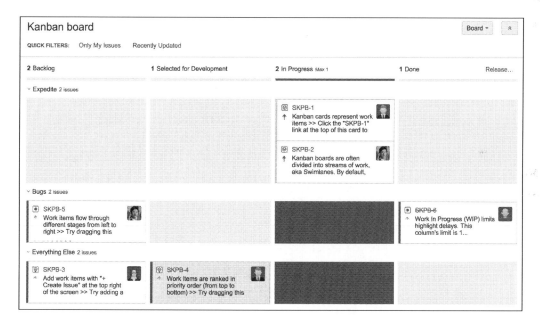

To customize swimlanes for your Kanban board, perform the following steps:

1. Go to the Kanban board that you want to customize swimlanes for.
2. Click on the **Board** dropdown menu and select the **Configure** option.

3. Select **Swimlanes** from the left navigation.

4. Choose the criteria you want to base your swimlane on in the **Base Swimlane on** field.

5. Create a new swimlane by entering the name and description for the swimlane, and enter the JQL query if you are basing your swimlanes on queries.

6. Reorder your swimlanes by dragging them up and down the list:

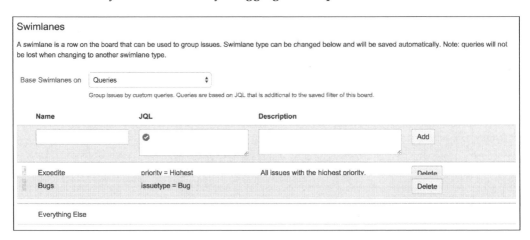

As shown in the preceding screenshot, we have three swimlanes based on queries. The **Expedite** and **Everything Else** swimlanes were there by default when we created the board. We have a new **Bugs** swimlane that is using the JQL query of issuetype = Bug, so all issues of the **Bug** type will be categorized together.

Note that the order of swimlanes is important. The order will determine both the placement of each swimlane and the swimlane an issue will belong to. In this case, the Expedite swimlane is on the top, so this will reflect in the final Kanban board. If we have an issue that is of the **Bug** type and also a value of **Highest** for the **priority** field, it will be categorized into the **Expedite** swimlane rather than the **Bugs** swimlane because of the order.

The JQL option is the most flexible way of defining swimlanes, but you can also use some of the built-in options such as **Assignee** for simpler purposes. The next screenshot shows a Kanban board with four swimlanes, each showing the issues for a user, so you easily get an idea of how many issues are assigned to each user:

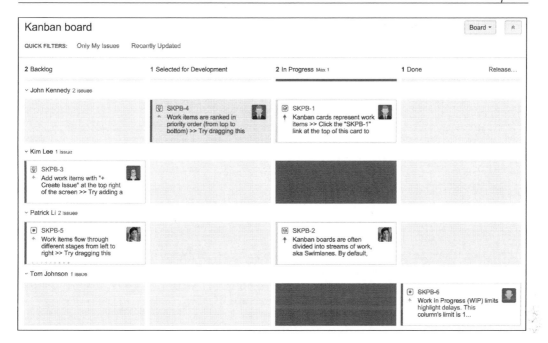

Creating custom views with quick filters

By default, the Kanban board will display all the issues that are returned from the selected filter. However, there might be times you need to do additional filtering on top, to narrow down the list of issues further. This is where quick filters come in.

Quick filters let you define additional filtering based on JQL. This is like creating a custom view for the board to include only the issues that you are interested to see for the time being. To create new quick filters, perform the following steps:

1. Go to the Kanban board you want to add quick filters to.
2. Click on the **Board** dropdown menu and select the **Configure** option.
3. Select **Quick Filters** from the left navigation.
4. Enter a name and description for the new quick filter.
5. Enter the JQL query for the filter. JIRA Agile will help you construct and validate the query.

6. Click on the **Add** button to create the new quick filter:

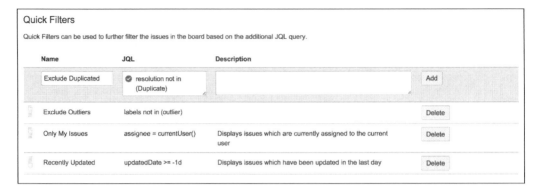

As shown in the preceding screenshot, we have three quick filters already created, and we are creating a new one named **Exclude Duplicated** with the JQL query of `resolution not in (Duplicate)`, to remove all issues with the value of **Duplicate** in the resolution field from the board.

Once you have created the new quick filters, they will be displayed above the issue cards, as shown in the following screenshot:

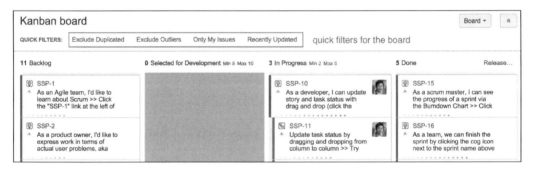

Releasing a version in Kanban

With Kanban, tasks are not assigned to a predefined or planned release schedule. Releases are made at the team's discretion, as more and more tasks are being completed. The idea here is to continuously release new features and improvements as and when it makes sense for the team. For example, some teams may choose to release based on a regular basis, such as every Friday. Other teams may choose to release based on they have completed something useful.

To release a version from your Kanban board, perform the following steps:

1. Click on the **Release...** link at the top right-hand corner of your board.

2. Enter the version number from the **Release** dialog.

3. Select the release date.

4. Enter a short description for the version.

5. Click on the **Release** button to release the version, as depicted in the following screenshot:

 You must have the **Administer Projects** permission for all projects included in the board, in order to release the version.

Once you have released a version, all the issues in the last column will have the version number added to their fix versions field, and be taken off the Kanban board.

One thing to note about versions when working in Kanban is that you should not create the version you want to release ahead of time.

It is important to note that with Kanban, the "release plan" is to be continuously optimized. There is no point in releasing something simply because of a rule that states a release needs to be made on a Friday, when there are not many completed tasks. The team needs to look at their current lead time, and then make the decision whether or not it makes sense to make a release.

Improving your team's performance

One common question that often pops up when teams are starting with Kanban is, "what is the correct limit I should set for each of my workflow statuses?" And the answer is simple; try and experiment.

The first step is to look at your board and see if any constraints are being violated. If we take a look at the following example of a Kanban board, we can see too many issues are in the **In Progress** column, and at the same time, we don't have enough issues in the **QA** column. What this tells us is we have a bottleneck in our development phase of the workflow. This results in work being piled up in development, while the QA engineers are waiting around and not being productive:

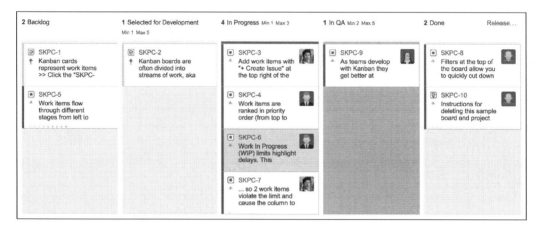

So in order to fix this, as a team you will need to take a close look at the bottleneck, in this case the **In Progress** column, and figure out why this is happening. For example, this can be either because you do not have enough developers to handle the workload, or the tasks are too complicated and need to be broken down.

Defining the column constraint can be an art, and once you have set the constraints, you will need to periodically review them and refine them as the project and team changes. When setting column constraints, keep the following points in mind:

- **Limit set too high**: You will have idle tasks sitting around, and this leads to bad lead/cycle time

- **Limit set too low**: You will have idle people waiting for work, and this leads to bad productivity

Remember, with Kanban, you and your team should continuously improve your process, look at the board and identify if there are any bottlenecks, look for the cause, and address it.

[Do not just fix the board, fix the cause of the bottleneck.]

Improving the process with charts and reports

JIRA Agile comes with a number of useful charts and reports to help you visualize your team's performance and identify potential bottlenecks in your Kanban process. To generate a report, perform the following steps:

1. Browse to the Kanban board you want to generate a report on.
2. Click on the **Reports** tab from the left panel of your board.

As shown in the following screenshot, there are a number of reports that are available. The reports under the **Agile** section are specifically designed for using agile methodologies such as Kanban. Of course, the other reports such as **Pie Chart Report** are also very useful, but since these are vanilla JIRA reports we will be focusing mainly on the agile reports, namely **Cumulative Flow Diagram**, and **Control Chart**:

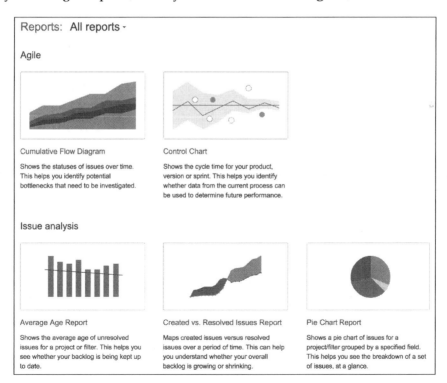

Cumulative flow diagram

The first useful chart JIRA Agile provides is the cumulative flow diagram. This chart shows you the number of issues (y axis) in various statuses, displayed as colored bands, over a period of time (x axis). This way, you will be able to visually identify if there are any bottlenecks in a particular status in your team's workflow, as you will see a widening in the colored band representing the status.

To generate the cumulative flow diagram for your Kanban board, perform the following steps:

1. Click on the **Reports** tab from the left panel of your board.

2. Select the **Cumulative Flow Diagram** option:

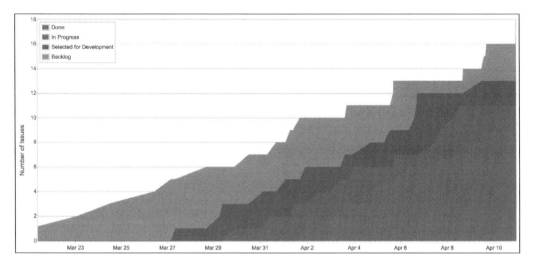

Control chart

The second useful chart, to help you measure your team's performance, is the control chart. The control chart shows you the average lead time of your team over a period of time, and plots the issues on the chart so you can see the following:

- Any issues that are outside of the standard deviation, also known as outliers

- The average time taken to complete tasks

- The team's rolling average and how it compares to the average

To generate the control chart for your Kanban board, perform the following steps:

1. Click on the **Reports** tab from the left panel of your board.
2. Select the **Control Chart** option.

As shown in the following screenshot, the control chart shows:

- Issues on the board represented by green dots. A hollow green dot represents a single issue and a solid green dot (bigger) represents multiple issues. You can click on these dots to see the issue details.

- The time period shown as dates, on the *x* axis.

- The duration it takes for issues to be completed, on the *y* axis.

- The average duration for issue completions shown as the red line.

- The average lead time for issues shown as the blue line. A downward trending blue line indicates improvements in efficiency.

- The standard deviation shown as a light blue band:

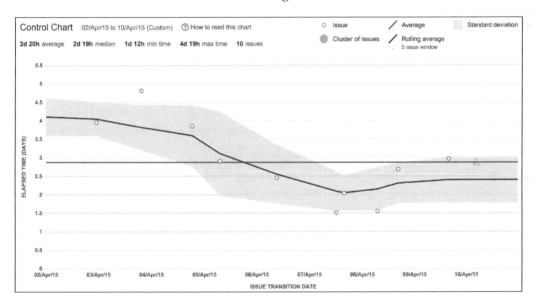

Generally, you would want to have the blue line trending downwards; this would indicate a decrease in the average lead time. This means issues are not stuck in workflow statuses and are being completed quickly, and that your team is not overbooked.

You would also want to have a low standard deviation. This is an indication of how each issue is measured against the rolling average (blue line). The narrower the blue band, the closer each issue is being delivered to the average time. This means that it's more likely the team will be able to deliver work in the same cadence.

Customizing the control chart

The control chart has several customization options that allow you to fine tune the data being displayed on the chart. These options are displayed below the chart itself, as shown in the following screenshot:

When you first start working with the control chart, you would want to identify and remove the outliers from the chart as they can often skew your data and give you incorrect readings.

Outliers are the green dots far above the light blue band; these are often issues that are created or transitioned incorrectly due to human error. You can easily filter out these issues by applying a label to each of the issues and creating a new quick filter. To do this, perform the following steps:

1. Review each outlying issue, and apply a label (outlier) to it if confirmed to be an outlier.
2. Create a new quick filter for the board with the following JQL: `labels not in (outlier)`.
3. Select the new quick filter from the **Quick Filters** field on the control chart.

You can use this technique to filter out other issues that might skew your chart, such as duplicated issues.

Summary

In this chapter, we looked at using JIRA Agile for Kanban. We have looked at the Kanban board and how to configure it to model your existing workflow, as well as setting up column constraints to limit work in progress, which is the key concept with Kanban. We have also looked at some of the charts available to help you identify potential bottlenecks in your process, so you and your team can work together to address those issues, and improve your process.

Now that we have covered using JIRA Agile for both Scrum and Kanban, we will look at some advanced features that can help you get more out of JIRA Agile.

5
JIRA Agile – Advanced

In the previous chapters, we looked at how to use JIRA Agile to run and manage projects with both Scrum and Kanban. In this chapter, we will look into some of the additional customization capabilities of JIRA Agile, as well as integrating with other systems to provide a complete end-to-end experience for you and your team.

By the end of the chapter, you will have learned how to:

- Customize Agile Cards for your board
- Run parallel sprints
- Display and share project information with dashboard
- Create and link epics to requirement pages
- Create user stories from requirement pages
- Display sprints on calendars
- Capture sprint meeting notes
- Share reports on project progress
- Print out your Agile Cards and pin them onto a physical board

Customizing Agile Cards

JIRA Agile displays issues and tasks as cards on your Scrum and Kanban boards. The default settings for a card contain just enough information, such as summary and assignee, to let users know what each card is talking about. JIRA Agile allows you to further customize how the Agile Cards should be displayed for each individual board, including its color and additional fields to display.

Customizing card color

You might have noticed that different cards have different color bars on their left-hand sides. By default, colors are assigned based on the card's issue type. JIRA Agile has four options to decide how color should be assigned to cards: **Issue Types**, **Priorities**, **Assignees**, and **Queries**.

With the first three options, JIRA Agile will automatically detect the available options based on your current board's setup. For example, if you select **Priorities**, JIRA Agile will list all the priority values available in the system, and all you have to do is select a color for each priority.

The **Queries** option is the most flexible option, where you can define any number of colors and use JQL queries as the condition. For example, you can assign colors to cards based on the issue's due dates, red if the issue needs to be finished in the next 24 hours, and green if it is not due until next week. This way, when you look at the board, you get an indicator of each issue's urgency in relation to time. To customize card color, perform the following:

1. Browse to the board you want to customize card colors for.
2. Click on the **Configure** option from the **Board** menu.
3. Select the **Card colors** option from the left panel.
4. Choose how you want to assign colors from the **Colors based on** select list.
5. Select the color for each criterion by clicking on the color box.

As shown in the following screenshot, we are assigning colors based on **Queries**, and all issues that are due within 1 day will have their cards shown in red, with the JQL query of `duedate <= "1d"`:

Once you have customized the color settings for your card, the changes will be applied immediately. The following screenshot shows the result of a board with customized color cards:

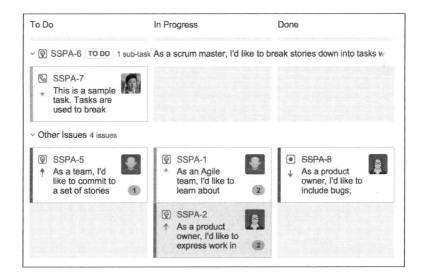

Customizing card layout

By default, each card shows only basic information about the task, such as its summary, assignee, and priority. This is usually enough for most cases of usage, however, if you have customized your JIRA instance, especially with custom fields, you might want to also display that information on the card.

JIRA Agile lets you add up to three additional fields on the Agile Cards, including custom fields. However, since the on-screen real estate is still limited, you need to make sure not to add fields such as description, which can make the card hard to read. To customize the card layout, perform the following steps:

1. Browse to the board you want to customize cards for.
2. Click on the **Configure** option from the **Board** menu.
3. Select the **Card layout** option from the left panel.
4. Choose the field you want to add from the **Field Name** list and click on the **Add** button.

Since you can only add a maximum of three fields, as soon as you have selected three fields to add, JIRA Agile will remove the **Field Name** select list automatically. Until you remove a field from the list, as we can see in the following screenshot, under the **Active sprints** section, the **Field Name** list is no longer available.

Also note that there are two sections, **Backlog** and **Active sprints** on the **Card layout** page. JIRA Agile lets you set two different sets of fields, so you have the flexibility to show different fields when issues are in backlog, and when they are moved into sprints:

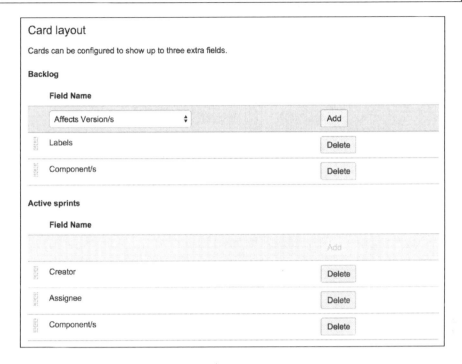

As shown in the following screenshot, we have added two additional fields to our cards, **Label (sample)** and **Components (Authentication, Database)**. For cards that do not have values for either of the two fields, the value **None** will be displayed, as in the case of issue **SKP-18**:

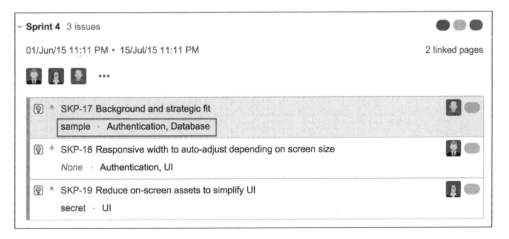

Customizing the card details view

In the previous section, we looked at how to customize the layout of cards by adding additional fields. JIRA Agile also lets you customize the issue's details view. The details view is the right-hand section when you select a card. By default, it will have all the default fields such as status and assignee. So, if you have any custom fields you would like to display, you will need to customize the view.

To customize the card details view, perform the following:

1. Browse to the board you want to customize card details view for.
2. Click the **Configure** option from the **Board** menu.
3. Select the **Issue Detail View** option from the left panel.
4. Add and remove fields for each view section.

As shown in the following screenshot, the configuration page is divided into several sections, corresponding to the actual details view panel. Each section can only have fields of compatible types. For example, only date-related fields can be added to the **Date Fields** section:

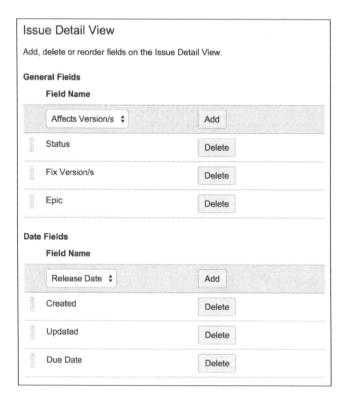

Once you have added or removed fields from the details view, whenever a user clicks on a card, the right-hand panel will reflect the change, as shown in the following screenshot, where we have removed the **Labels**, **Component/s**, and **Affects Version/s** fields, and added the **Due Date** field:

Running parallel sprints with Scrum

By default, JIRA Agile lets you have only one active sprint with Scrum, which is how it works. The team works on only one sprint at a time and moves onto the next sprint once the current one is delivered. However, if you have multiple teams working on the same project, and sharing the same backlog, you will need to be able to have multiple sprints running in parallel.

JIRA Agile has the ability to support parallel sprints via its labs features. Labs features are features that are in the beta testing phase. While they might be fully functional, they are not supported and are subject to future changes, so use them with care.

To enable the parallel sprints feature, perform the following steps:

1. Click on the cog icon at the top right-hand corner of the screen and select the **Add-ons** option.

2. Select the **JIRA Agile Labs** option from the left navigation panel.

3. Check the **Parallel Sprints** option.

Once you have enabled parallel sprints, you can then go to any Scrum board, create a few sprints, and you will see the **Start Sprint** button is available to all sprints, even if there is already an active sprint. This is shown in the following screenshot:

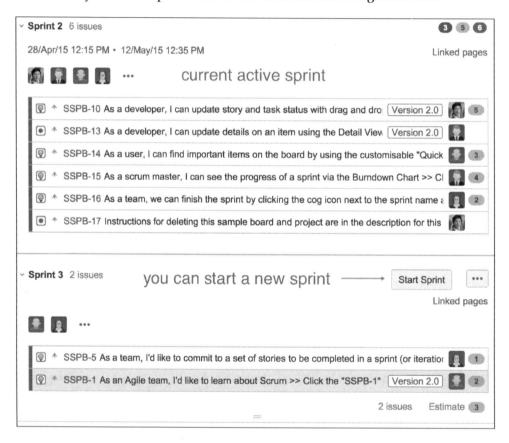

Displaying JIRA Agile reports

As we have seen in *Chapter 2, JIRA Agile for Scrum*, and *Chapter 4, JIRA Agile for Kanban*, JIRA Agile comes with a number of reports that you can generate to get a better understanding of how your project is tracking. However, they often require you to go to your board and then generate the report manually. A better way to display and share information on your project is to take advantage of some of JIRA's built-in features. Remember, JIRA Agile is an add-on for JIRA, so you have access to many of JIRA's powerful capabilities.

Using the JIRA dashboard

The easiest way to display and share your project and sprint progress with everyone is to use the dashboard feature from JIRA. A dashboard acts as a portal page for your project, and you can display different information about your project by adding gadgets onto the dashboard.

JIRA Agile comes with a number of gadgets that are designed specifically to display agile related information, including:

- **Sprint burndown gadget**: This displays a burndown chart of your sprint on the dashboard. The chart will be automatically updated to reflect the current data.

- **Days remaining in sprint gadget**: This displays how many days are left before the sprint is scheduled to complete, and acts as a reminder for how much time is left on the clock.

- **Sprint health gadget**: This displays a bar chart showing information on how the sprint is progressing, for example, how much more work is still left to do.

The power of using JIRA dashboard is that you are not limited to use only the gadgets that are provided by JIRA Agile. JIRA comes with many other useful gadgets that you can use to drill down into your project and sprint. They are as follows:

- **Filter results gadget**: You can select a filter and display the result in a table. You can use this to display the most important issues in the sprint.

- **Two dimensional filter statistics gadget**: This is similar to the filter results gadget, but instead of displaying a list of issues, it will display a statistical breakdown of the filter result based on the fields you choose.

- **Pie chart gadget**: You can select a filter and the result will be displayed as a pie chart, where each slice is based on a field of your choice, for example, priority.

As you can see, you can build a very useful dashboard by combining gadgets from JIRA Agile and gadgets from JIRA itself. You can even create your own gadget or download gadgets from third-party vendors to display information specific to your need.

To create a dashboard for your project and sprint, perform the following steps:

1. Select the **Manage Dashboards** option from the **Dashboards** menu.
2. Click on the **Create new dashboard** button.
3. Enter a name for your new dashboard.
4. Select how you want to share the dashboard. Dashboards are private by default, so for others to see the dashboard, you must share the dashboard with them. As shown in the following screenshot, we are sharing the dashboard with members of the **Top Secret Project**.
5. Click on the **Add** button to create the dashboard:

 Make sure you click on the **Add** button after you have selected who to share the dashboard with.

Once you have created a new dashboard, you can start adding contents onto it with gadgets:

1. Click on the **Add a new gadget** link. It does not matter which one you click, as you can always re-position the gadgets after they have been added, by simply dragging them around on the dashboard.

2. Select the gadgets you want to add from the **Add a gadget** dialog by clicking on its **Add gadget** button. If you want to add only JIRA Agile specific gadgets, type in the word agile in the search box, as shown in the following screenshot.

3. Close the dialog once you have added all the gadgets you want:

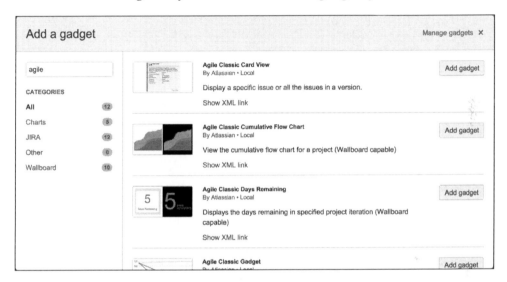

Once you have added the gadgets, you will need to configure each gadget to display the data you want. For most gadgets, all you need to do is select the board, sprint, project, or filter to use:

You can also configure the layout of the dashboard. By default, the dashboard is divided into two columns of equal width. You can change that by clicking on the **Edit Layout** button and then selecting the layout you want.

Using wallboard

Another great JIRA feature you can take advantage of is the wallboard. You can think of wallboards as JIRA dashboards that you display on a big wall using a projector, or with a big monitor.

Using wallboard is a great way to share information about your project with your team and other colleagues. The following screenshot shows an example of a wallboard. By taking the data out of JIRA Agile, and projecting that onto a big screen, everyone will have instant and easy access to the information they need. As people walk by your team's work area, they will get a good idea on how the team is progressing:

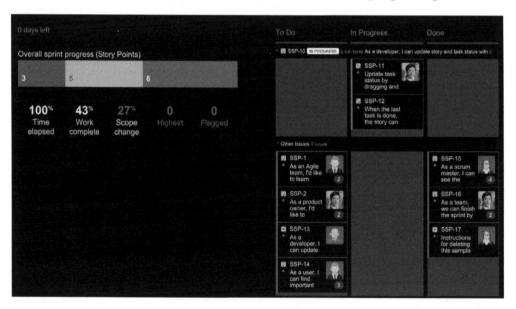

To set up a wallboard for your agile project, you will first need to create a dashboard. Note that not all gadgets are wallboard compatible, but all the agile gadgets that come with JIRA Agile are compatible. Once you have your dashboard ready, click on the **Tools** menu and select the **View as Wallboard** option, link it up to a big monitor, and you have yourself an awesome wallboard.

If you have multiple dashboards, you can create a slideshow of wallboards. All you have to do is select the **Set up Wallboard Slideshow** option from the **Tools** menu, as shown in the following screenshot, to set up the slideshow. Select the dashboards to include on the wall, how you would like the slideshow to look (**Display Options**), and use the **View as Wallboard Slideshow** option to display it:

Integrating JIRA Agile with Confluence

As we have seen, JIRA Agile is able to leverage many JIRA features to add more value to simply running and managing your tasks on a board. Another great tool JIRA Agile integrates with very tightly is Confluence.

Confluence is a team collaboration solution from Atlassian (the maker of JIRA and JIRA Agile) that enables teams to collaborate and create content together. Organizations often use it to create and share information related to projects such as functional and design specifications. JIRA Agile works seamlessly with Confluence to provide you with a complete agile experience. In the following sections, we will look at how you can integrate JIRA Agile with Confluence to:

- Create epics and user stories with design documentation
- Manage and view your sprints on a calendar
- Capture meeting notes for your sprint planning sessions
- Create retrospective reports at the end of each sprint
- Share and publish release information

Setting up an application link with Confluence

If you have not already integrated JIRA and Confluence together, you need to create a new application link. To create an application link with Confluence, perform the following steps:

1. Click on the cog icon from top right-hand corner and select the **Add-ons** option.

2. Select the **Application Links** option from the left navigation panel.

3. Enter the URL to your Confluence instance and click on the **Create new link** button, as show in the next screenshot:

Configure Application Links ⑦

You have no application links right now. To create an application link begin by entering the URL of application you wish to link to.

Application http://wiki.localhost.com:8090   Create new link

4. Tick the **The servers have the same set of users and usernames** option if both JIRA and Confluence share the same user repository, for example, LDAP.

> If you have a common user repository for both applications, such as LDAP, by enabling this option, users will have a seamless experience. Otherwise, they will be prompted to authorize access for the first time viewing of contents from the other application.

5. Tick the **I am an administrator on both instances** option if you have an administrator account on both JIRA and Confluence. This will let you also create a reciprocal link from Confluence to JIRA.

6. Click on the **Continue** button:

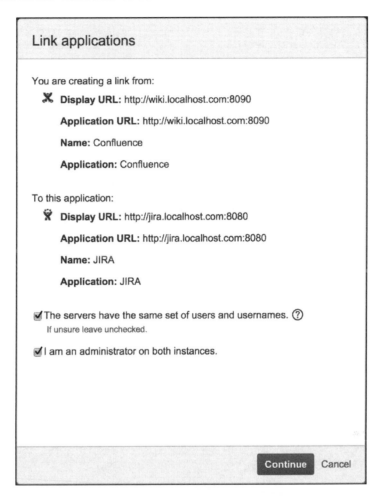

7. Verify that the onscreen information is correct. If both applications are able to communicate with each other successfully, it will display the URLs and application name and type, as shown in the following screenshot. Then, click on the **Continue** button:

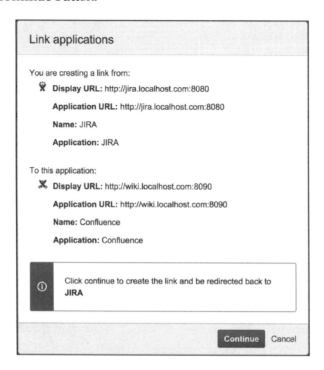

8. Continue with the onscreen wizard, and once the application link is successfully created, you will see a success message and the new application link listed for Confluence:

Creating Confluence pages from epics

JIRA Agile is a great tool to track and manage your day-to-day activities for your project, but it is not the best tool to capture detailed information for your tasks, such as design documentation and functional specifications for your epics.

With Confluence as a documentation platform, there are a few ways you can create design documents and link them to your epics.

The first option is to create your documents called Confluence pages, directly from your backlog:

1. Browse to your Scrum board and go to its backlog.
2. Open up the **Epics** panel from the left-hand side.
3. Select and expand the epic you want to create a Confluence page for.
4. Click on the **Links pages** link from the epic.
5. Click on the **Create page** button from the dialog, as shown in the following screenshot:

After you click on the **Create page** button, you will be taken to Confluence in a new browser tab with the **Create** dialog displayed, as shown in the following screenshot. By default, the dialog will have the **Project requirements** template (also called blueprint) pre-selected for you, but you can choose to use a different template if you want. Also note that the **Select space** field at the top will have the last Confluence space you have visited pre-selected, so make sure you select the correct space to create your new page in.

6. Click on the **Create** button after you have selected the correct space to create your new page in:

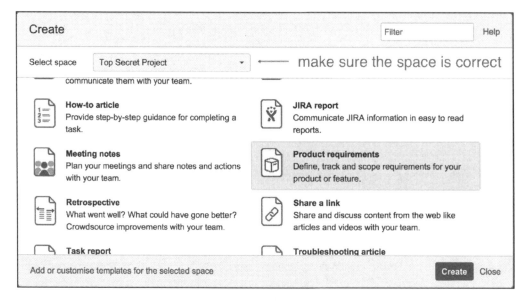

7. If this is the first time you have used the product requirements template, you will get a **Let's get started** information dialog, as seen in the following screenshot. Simply tick the **Don't show this again** option at the bottom and click on the **Create** button to create your new page:

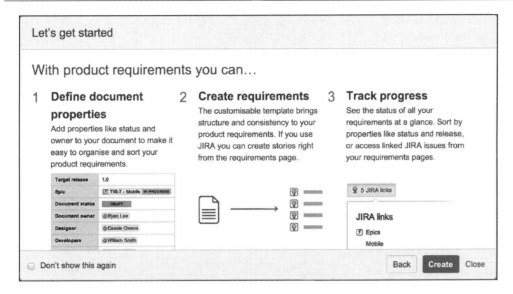

8. Click on the **Create** button again to start working on the new page.

Confluence will present you with a new page and editor, with a pre-defined template. You can simply fill in the templates with information such as goals and requirements. A few important things to note:

- Make sure you give your page a title. A good practice is to name it after the linked epic.

- Reference the epic in JIRA by clicking on the **Link to related JIRA epic of feature** text label from the **Epic** field. This way, a reference link will be created between the requirement page and the epic issue.

With the page created, if you go back to JIRA, the **Linked pages** link for the epic will change to **1 linked page**, and clicking on that will show you the actual linked page, as shown in the following screenshot:

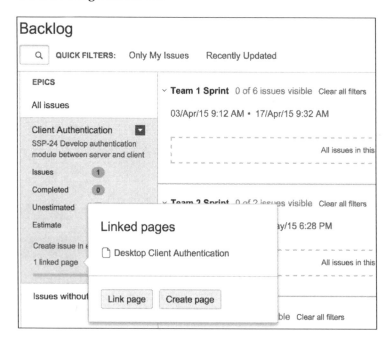

If you already have requirement pages created for the project, instead of creating new ones from the epics, you can simply link to those pages by clicking on the **Link page** button. After clicking on it, you will get a search box, and you can type in your page's title, find the page you want, and select it to create a link. This is illustrated in the next screenshot:

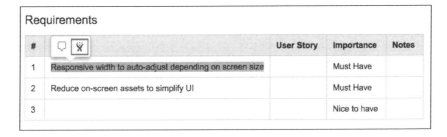

[If you cannot see the linked pages, make sure Confluence
has remote API enabled. See `https://confluence.
atlassian.com/x/vEsC` for more details.]

Creating user stories from Confluence

If you are using the product requirements blueprint, as we have seen earlier, there
is a section on the page for you to list out all the requirements for the feature. Once
you have defined all the requirements with the team, you can create JIRA Agile user
stories directly on the page. To do this, perform the following steps:

1. Go to your product requirements page in Confluence.

2. Highlight the text of the requirement you want to create a user story with.
   The text you highlight will become the summary of the user story, as shown
   in the following screenshot:

#				User Story	Importance	Notes
1		Responsive width to auto-adjust depending on screen size			Must Have	
2		Reduce on-screen assets to simplify UI			Must Have	
3					Nice to have	

3. Click the JIRA icon. This will open up the **Create Issue** dialog, as shown in the following screenshot.

4. Make sure the project and issue type selection is correct. You can click on the **Edit** link to change that.

5. Enter a description for the user story.

6. If the Product Requirements page is already linked to an epic in JIRA Agile, you will see a **Link to epic** option. Uncheck this option if you do not want the user story to be added to the epic.

7. Click on the **Create** button to create the user story:

If you have multiple requirements listed in the Requirements table on your page, you can click on the **Create x issues from this table** option at the bottom, and Confluence will automatically create a user story for each requirement you have.

After you have created the user stories, you will see a JIRA issue added next to each of the requirements, showing their key and status. Their status will be automatically updated as the issues are being worked on. You will also see a **JIRA links** button at the top of the page next to the breadcrumbs. Clicking on that will display all the JIRA issues currently linked to this page, including any epics and user stories. Refer to the following screenshot:

 Currently, the JIRA links button is only available if you use the default theme in Confluence.

Planning your sprints with Team Calendar

As you and your team work on the sprint, it is often helpful to see how your sprints fit in with other activities your team might have. For example, if there are team members going on a vacation or having travel plans half way through a sprint, or if there are other delivery commitments that might interfere with the sprint.

Again, the key to solve this is to have all this information visually displayed on a single calendar, viewable and shared by the entire team, so everyone can stay well informed, just like having tasks plotted on an agile board. To do this, perform the following steps:

1. Browse to your team's **Team Calendar**.
2. Click on the **Add Event** button.
3. Select the **JIRA Agile Sprints** option for **Event Type**:

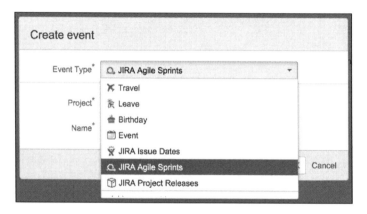

4. Select the project that belongs to your Scrum board.
5. Enter a name for the event.
6. Click on the **OK** button to create the event.

Once you have created the event, Team Calendar will get all the sprints you have for the selected project, and display them on the calendar. As shown in the following screenshot, we have two sprints, **Sprint 2** and **Sprint 3**. We can also see that **Tom Johnson** will be away at the start of **Sprint 2**, which might have an impact on the team's ability to complete everything in the sprint on time. Also, if you have all team members' vacation plans on the calendar, then during your sprint planning sessions, you will have all the information you need when deciding how much work should go into the sprint and how long the sprint should be:

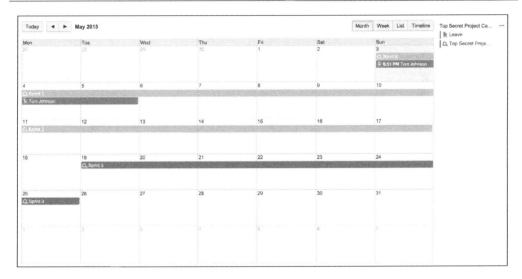

With the calendar all set up, you can also share and embed it. A good way to use this feature is to create a new Confluence page in the same project space where you have all your requirement documentation, call it something like **Project Calendar**, and then embed the calendar into the page. To embed the calendar into a page:

1. Click on the **Create** button at the top of the page.
2. Select the project space for the **Select space** field.
3. Now select the **Blank page** option and click on the **Create** button.
4. Name the page **Project Calendar**.
5. Select and add the **Team Calendar** macro into the page.
6. Click on the **Add Existing Calendar** option.
7. Search for the calendar you have created, and click on the **Add** button.

8. Click on the **Save** button to create the page:

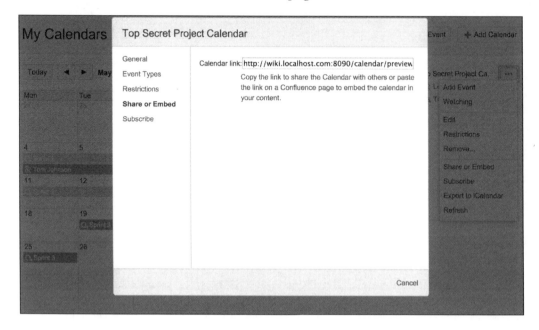

After you have created the page, you will have all the information about the project in a single place, along with the Confluence space for the project, for easy access. One additional step you can take is to create a quick shortcut link on your Scrum board to the Project Calendar page, so it is just a click away when you need it.

To create a link to the page:

1. Browse to your Scrum board.
2. Click on the **Add link** option from the left-hand side.
3. Enter the URL for the **Project Calendar** page.
4. Enter a label for the link, that is, **Project Calendar**.
5. Click on the **Add** button to create the link.

The link will be displayed under the **Project Shortcuts** section on the left-hand side, as shown in the following screenshot. So during your sprint planning sessions, or work sessions on the active sprint, you can easily access **Project Calendar** and get the most up-to-date information:

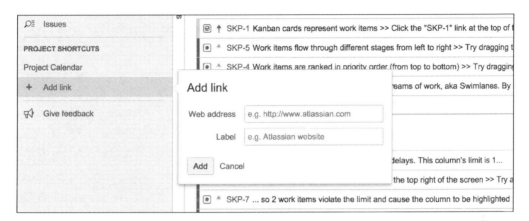

Capturing sprint meeting notes

As we have seen, you can plan and visualize your sprints with Confluence's Team Calendar. Another important part of your sprint planning session is to keep records of the meetings, capturing what was discussed, decisions made, and being able to reference back to those meeting notes in the context of your sprints.

Just like requirement documents, Confluence is also a great place to capture and store this information. From inside your Scrum board, you can create and link each sprint to pages in Confluence, just like with epics.

To create a meeting note for a sprint:

1. Browse to your Scrum board.
2. Click on **Backlog** on the left-hand side to display all your sprints.
3. Click on the **Linked pages** link for the sprint that you want to create a meeting note for.

4. Click on the **Create page** button if you want to create a new meeting note page, or the **Link page** button if you already have the meeting note ready:

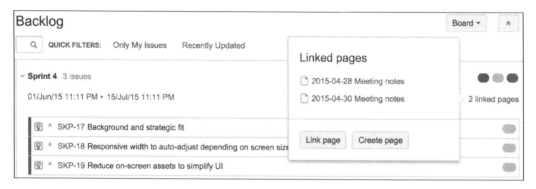

If you click on the **Create page** button, you will be taken to Confluence, with the **Create** dialog showing. It will have the **Meeting notes** blueprint pre-selected. Make sure the correct space is selected and click on the **Create** button; you will be able to start entering your meeting information. Once you have created and saved the meeting note, the page will have a JIRA link referencing the sprint it has been created for, as shown in the following screenshot, and the sprint will also list all the meeting notes it has:

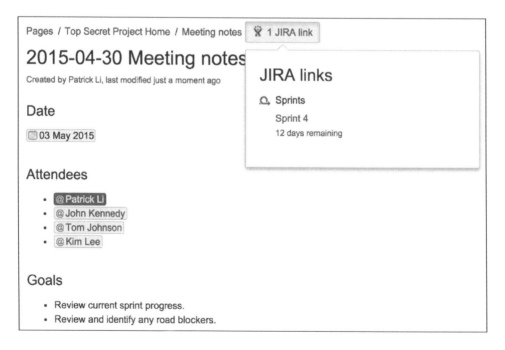

Creating retrospective reports

Other than creating meeting notes, another great feature is being able to create retrospective sprint reports at the end of each sprint. Remember, one of the key ideas behind agile is continuous improvement, so it is important that at the end of each sprint, the entire team comes together and discusses what they did well, and what went wrong during the sprint; also, to summarize lessons learnt, and discuss how to improve the process in the next sprint as a team.

To create a retrospective report for your sprint, perform the following steps:

1. Browse to your Scrum board.
2. Click on **Reports** from the left-hand side.
3. Select the sprint to be reported on and select **Sprint Report**.
4. Click on the **Linked pages** link.
5. Click on the **Create page** button:

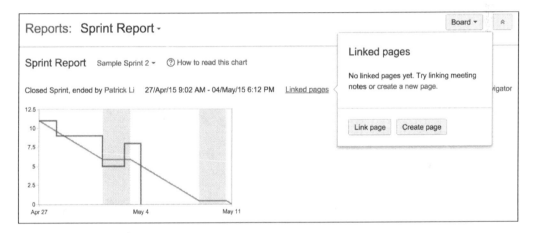

6. Click on the **Next** button in the Confluence **Create** dialog.
7. Enter a title for the report or leave the default.
8. Add all the team members present in the retrospective meeting.
9. Click on the **Create** button to start work on the report.

Just like all other reports created with JIRA Agile, a reference link will be created between the report and the sprint, so you can easily go back and forth between the two.

Displaying your project in Confluence

The last integration feature between JIRA Agile and Confluence is to create reports on the project based on specific versions. There are two types of reports you can create:

- **Change log report**: The change log report lists out all the issues that are part of a selected version. This saves you the hassle of manually compiling a list of issues and entering them. This is a great way to communicate changes within a given version to your customers and other stakeholders.

- **Status report**: The status report is a live report that shows the status of the project in a number of pie charts.

To create these reports, you will start in Confluence instead of JIRA Agile:

1. Log in to Confluence and browse to your project space.

2. Click on the **Create** button at the top or press the C key on your keyboard.

3. Select **JIRA Report** from the **Create** dialog and click on **Create**.

4. Choose the report you want to create and click the **Next** button. In our example, we are creating a status report:

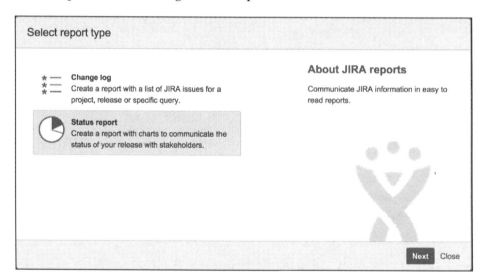

5. Select the project and version to report on. These fields are auto populated based on data coming from JIRA.

6. Enter a title for the report.

7. Click on the **Create** button to start work on the report.

The default report template will be auto populated based on the information you have provided, so you can simply click on the **Save** button to create the report without any further changes. The following screenshot shows a default status report:

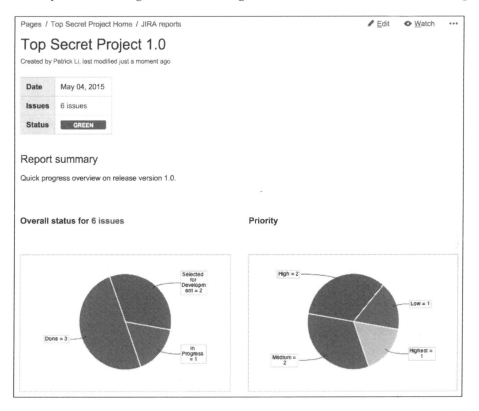

Working with JIRA Agile offline

JIRA Agile brings the power of agile to a web-based system where progress and reports can be accessed and shared with everyone, even if they aren't physically co-located together. However, sometimes it is still useful to have a physical board and cards so meetings such as daily stand-ups can feel more interactive and refreshing, rather than having everyone stare at a computer monitor all the time.

This can be done with a third-party add-on called Agile Cards for JIRA. You can search and install it from the UPM, in the same way you install JIRA Agile as explained in *Chapter 1, JIRA Agile Basics*, or download it from the following link, and upload it to JIRA:

```
https://marketplace.atlassian.com/plugins/com.spartez.scrumprint.
scrumplugin
```

Once you have installed the Agile Cards add-on, you will see a new print icon added to your boards. The following screenshot shows the new icon in the **Backlog** view of a Scrum board. The icon is also available in the **Active** sprints mode and on Kanban board:

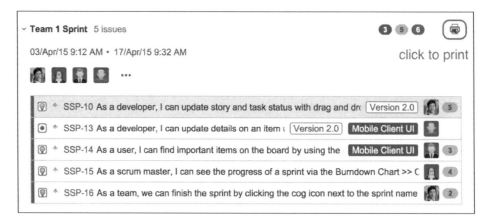

> The print function is also available outside of JIRA Agile, for example, when you run a search in issue navigator, or when viewing individual issues.

When you click on the print icon, a new tab will be opened, and each issue will be turned into a card, as shown in the following screenshot:

After you have printed your Agile Cards, you can cut them up and pin them onto your physical board, and use them in your team meetings.

After all, printing out your tasks and pinning them on a board is only half the story; you would need to import all these changes back into JIRA Agile at then end of your meetings. The Agile Cards add-on does just that, by letting you take a photo of your board, and then import that back into JIRA Agile.

Now, the first thing you need to do is make a change to your print layout to include column information for your cards. To do this, perform the following steps:

1. Browse to the JIRA administration console and select the **Add-ons** tab.

2. Select the **Settings** option from the left-hand side navigation, under the **AGILE CARDS** heading.

3. Click on the **Edit** link for the default template (unless you have created custom templates, in which case you should edit your own template).

4. Click on the **Simple Layout** tab.

5. Select the **KR code – for Board Scanner** option from the **Upper-left image** field.

6. Click on the **Save** button to update your settings.

With this change, when you print your Agile Cards, you will see a different code marking on the left-hand side of your cards, as shown in the screenshot that follows. This is very important as these markings contain each card's current column information:

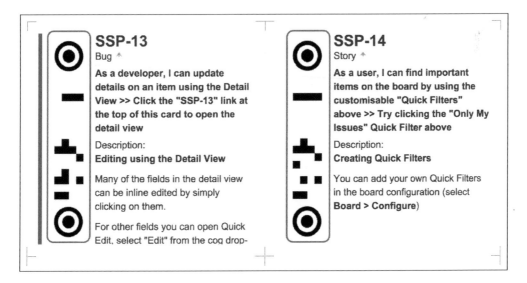

Now that you have added column information to your card printouts, the next thing you need to do is print out a few more items to help Agile Cards better process your photo. Perform the following steps:

1. Browse to the Scrum or Kanban board where you have printed your Agile Cards.

2. Expand the **Add-ons** section and select the **Agile Cards: Define Task Board Layout** option, as shown in the following screenshot:

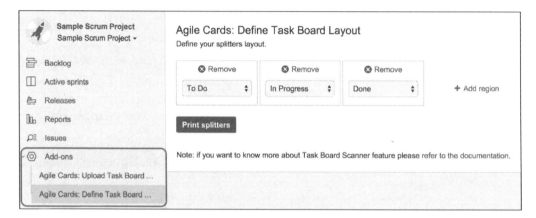

3. Set up the board layout to mimic your physical board—which should have the same set up as your JIRA Agile board—by clicking on the **Add region** link. You should have one region per board column.

 Your physical board and JIRA Agile board need to have the same column setup in order for Agile Cards to process your photo.

4. Click on the **Print splitters** button. This will open up a new tab, with a new image called **splitters** for you to print. A splitter is a piece of paper you need to place between each column you have, so if you have three columns, two splitters will be generated.

5. Pin the splitter images onto your physical board, as shown in the following image. This will help Agile Cards to determine which column each card belongs to:

6. Take a photo off your board, and send it to your computer.

7. Select the **Agile Cards: Upload Task Board Photo** option.

8. Click on the **Upload Photo** button, and select the photo from step 7. If the photo is processed successfully, you will get a summary of all the changes, as shown in the following screenshot.

9. Review the result and click on the **automatically change status** link to update all issues, or the **bulk edit** links for each column and process them individually:

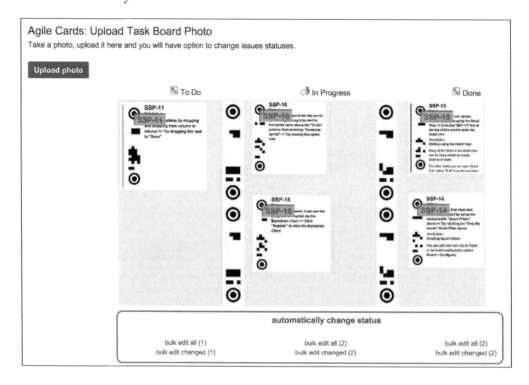

Agile Cards has several other customization options, such as letting you customize the layout of your card so you can decide what fields will be included in the printout. You can find out more at https://confluence.spartez.com/x/GwAt.

Summary

In this chapter, we looked at some of the additional customizations JIRA Agile offers, so you can now create your Scrum and Kanban boards just the way you want them. We also looked at JIRA Agile lab features, specifically parallel sprints. You need to take care when using these features in production, as they are generally not supported, and can be removed at any time.

JIRA Agile being an add-on for JIRA, is able to take full advantage of many JIRA features including the dashboard and wallboard, as well as the ability to integrate with other systems. We looked at integrating JIRA Agile with Confluence and Team Calendar, so you can create detailed documentations and report and cross reference them with epics, user stories, and sprints.

Remember, a bit part of these integrations is to take the data out of JIRA Agile so it is not in a silo, and share the information with the team and other stakeholders of your projects. By sharing information on a dashboard, and retrospectively reviewing your progress as a team, you can contiguously refine and improve together, and become successful at using agile and being agile.

Index

Thank you for buying

JIRA Agile Essentials

About Packt Publishing

Packt, pronounced 'packed', published its first book, *Mastering phpMyAdmin for Effective MySQL Management*, in April 2004, and subsequently continued to specialize in publishing highly focused books on specific technologies and solutions.

Our books and publications share the experiences of your fellow IT professionals in adapting and customizing today's systems, applications, and frameworks. Our solution-based books give you the knowledge and power to customize the software and technologies you're using to get the job done. Packt books are more specific and less general than the IT books you have seen in the past. Our unique business model allows us to bring you more focused information, giving you more of what you need to know, and less of what you don't.

Packt is a modern yet unique publishing company that focuses on producing quality, cutting-edge books for communities of developers, administrators, and newbies alike. For more information, please visit our website at www.packtpub.com.

About Packt Enterprise

In 2010, Packt launched two new brands, Packt Enterprise and Packt Open Source, in order to continue its focus on specialization. This book is part of the Packt Enterprise brand, home to books published on enterprise software – software created by major vendors, including (but not limited to) IBM, Microsoft, and Oracle, often for use in other corporations. Its titles will offer information relevant to a range of users of this software, including administrators, developers, architects, and end users.

Writing for Packt

We welcome all inquiries from people who are interested in authoring. Book proposals should be sent to author@packtpub.com. If your book idea is still at an early stage and you would like to discuss it first before writing a formal book proposal, then please contact us; one of our commissioning editors will get in touch with you.

We're not just looking for published authors; if you have strong technical skills but no writing experience, our experienced editors can help you develop a writing career, or simply get some additional reward for your expertise.

JIRA Essentials

Third Edition

ISBN: 978-1-78439-812-5   Paperback: 390 pages

Use the features of JIRA to manage projects and effectively handle bugs and software issues

1. Install, build, and implement your own Atlassian JIRA instance to track and manage projects.

2. Customize your JIRA with data capture and display, workflow design, and security to suit your requirements.

3. Step-by-step exercises at the end of each chapter for you to try out and reinforce your skills.

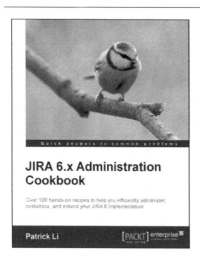

JIRA 6.x Administration Cookbook

ISBN: 978-1-78217-686-2   Paperback: 260 pages

Over 100 hands-on recipes to help you efficiently administer, customize, and extend your JIRA 6 implementation

1. Make JIRA adapt to your organization and process flow.

2. Gather and display the right information from users with customized forms and layouts.

3. Extend the capabilities of JIRA with add-ons, scripts, and integrations with other popular applications and cloud platforms.

Please check **www.PacktPub.com** for information on our titles

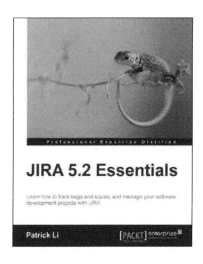

JIRA 5.2 Essentials

ISBN: 978-1-78217-999-3   Paperback: 396 pages

Learn how to track bugs and issues, and manage your software development projects with JIRA

1. Learn how to set up JIRA for software development.

2. Effectively manage and handle software bugs and issues.

3. Includes updated JIRA content as well as coverage of the popular GreenHopper plugin.

Agile Project Management with GreenHopper 6 Blueprints

ISBN: 978-1-84969-973-0   Paperback: 140 pages

An intuitive guide to efficiently track and manage projects in an agile way using GreenHopper for JIRA

1. Manage multi-project and multi-team backlog items for agile projects.

2. Learn how to use GreenHopper's rich interface features to focus on the work at hand and increase productivity.

3. Easy agile process adoption with pre-sets for Scrum & Kanban.

Please check **www.PacktPub.com** for information on our titles

Made in the USA
San Bernardino, CA
10 July 2020